Consoling Thoughts

of

St. Francis de Sales

—Third Book—

Consoling Thoughts on Sickness and Death

CONSOLING THOUGHTS
of
ST. FRANCIS DE SALES

—THIRD BOOK—

Consoling Thoughts on Sickness and Death

Gathered from His Writings,
And Arranged in Order, by the
REV. PÈRE HUGUET

TRANSLATED FROM THE FRENCH

27TH EDITION

"You cannot read anything more useful than the works of
St. Francis de Sales, in which everything is pleasing
and consoling."—Fenelon

TAN Books
An Imprint of Saint Benedict Press, LLC
Charlotte, North Carolina

Published by Fr. Pustet & Co., New York & Cincinnati, Printer to the Holy See and the S. Congregation of Rites, in 1912, under the title *The Consoling Thoughts of St. Francis de Sales*. A French edition of this work, apparently an earlier edition, was published in Paris in 1857 as *Pensees consolantes de Saint Francois de Sales*. . . . The compiler's surname is sometimes spelled Hoguet; his first name was given as Paul in the French edition. Retypeset in 2013 by TAN Books.

Cover design by Caroline Kiser.

Cover image: *Extreme Unction*, c.1637–40 (oil on canvas), Poussin, Nicolas (1594–1665) / National Gallery, London, UK / The Bridgeman Art Library

ISBN: 978-0-89555-218-1

Printed and bound in the United States of America.

TAN Books
An Imprint of Saint Benedict Press, LLC
Charlotte, North Carolina
2013

St. Francis de Sales' Loving Heart

"Through a great part of my soul I am poor and weak, but I have a boundless and almost immutable affection for those who favor me with their friendship. Whoever challenges me in the contest of friendship must be very determined, for I spare no effort. There is no person in the world who has a heart more tender and affectionate towards his friends than I, or one who feels a separation more acutely."
—St. Francis de Sales.

"It has pleased God to make my heart thus. I wish to love this dear neighbor ever so much—ever so much I wish to love him! Oh! When shall we be all melted away in meekness and charity towards our neighbor! I have given him my whole person, my means, my affections, that they may serve him in all his wants."—St. Francis de Sales.

CONTENTS

Publisher's Preface

S T. FRANCIS de Sales was a man of great passion. Reading his thought is to know his heart. Has Holy Mother Church ever reared a child so willing and able to express his longing for perfect union with God? Has a man so learned ever presented Truth and Beauty so simply?

Words cannot fully express the Publisher's appreciation for this Gentle Saint, the Bishop of Geneva and Doctor of the Church. Saint Francis was a lawyer, a theologian, and a missionary. As a young priest, he volunteered to re-evangelize the Calvinist of Chablais, France. He preached not only with conviction, but also with unparalleled gentleness and grace. He worked tirelessly, even under the cover of night, slipping his apologetic writings beneath the doors of anti-Catholics. The Lord rewarded him with one of the most remarkable and well-documented events in Catholic history when nearly the entire population of 72,000 Calvinists returned to the Faith.

This volume, *Consoling Thoughts*, is representative of why St. Francis was so well-received in Chablais, and indeed, throughout history. Perhaps more than any other saint, St. Francis preached truth with love. His teachings, his works, and his very presence were consoling to those 72,000 lost souls of Chablais and to millions of more over the centuries. Now, then, it is our hope that they will offer consolation to a new generation of Catholics.

It is for this reason that TAN Books is proud to bring this compilation of St. Francis' writings back to print. Initially published in a single volume, we now present this work in a four volume series, carefully arranged by topic to give solace in times of darkness, or, simply in times of deep meditation.

It is the Publisher's sincere hope that *Consoling Thoughts* finds a permanent home in your library and among our long list of Saint Francis de Sales classics, including *Introduction to the Devout Life*, *Treatise on the Love of God*, *Catholic Controversies*, and *Sermons of St. Francis de Sales* (in four volumes).

Saint Francis de Sales, Doctor of the Church, *Pray For Us*.

ROBERT M. GALLAGHER, PUBLISHER
November 19, 2012

Preface to the Sixth French Edition

By Père Huguet

SIX editions of this little work, published in a short time, tell better than any words of ours the popularity which St. Francis de Sales enjoys amongst us. Many sick and wounded souls have found in these sweet and affecting pages a heavenly consolation.

Encouraged by this success, the honor of which belongs to God and His blessed servant, we have again with pen in hand run through the works of the Bishop of Geneva, to glean carefully whatever had escaped us on our former tour. Nor has our labor been in vain; we have gathered new flowers, whose beauty and perfume yield in no respect to the first.[1] To introduce them in this edition, we have been obliged to lop off a good many of the old chapters which were so well suited to the object of the book. We have acted thus with the less regret as we have published the omitted

---

1 The author has scarcely taken anything from the *Introduction to a Devout Life,* this admirable book being in the hands of everyone.

portions, complete, in two other volumes: the *Consoling Piety of St. Francis de Sales,* and the *Month of Immaculate Mary, by St. Francis de Sales.* These two works form a complete course of consolation for all the trials of life.

We may be permitted to give a short extract from a late number of the *Catholic Bibliography,* which contained an article on *Consoling Thoughts.* The idea of publishing the article was most remote from our mind, on account of the many marks of very great kindness towards us which it bears; but remembering that the merit of this work belongs entirely to St. Francis de Sales, we have felt impelled to give at least an extract, as a new and encouraging proof of the opportuneness of our little book.

"The very title of the book," it says "pleases, and should secure a large number of readers. How many souls are there today who stand in need of being encouraged and consoled? Want of confidence is the great obstacle in the work of the Christian apostleship. Discouragement is the evil of our period, because in general the Christian life, or SANCTITY, appears like a sharp mountain, which only few persons can ascend; in despair of arriving at its summit the majority of men remain below on the plains. The mere word 'sanctity' frightens. The *Lives of the Saints,* which ought to encourage, often discourage, by their list of heroic virtues; we gladly conclude that such a state of perfection is suited only to a very small number, and we remain out of the ways of sanctity for fear of not being able to walk in them.

"Blessed then be the pious author who has received the happy inspiration of assembling together the *Consoling Thoughts of St. Francis de Sales,* the sweetest and most amiable of the saints, and one of the greatest masters of the spiritual life!

"It is especially by his admirable union of firmness and mildness that St. Francis de Sales shines in the first rank of ascetic writers. Who else ever painted virtue under lovelier colors, or made it easier or more practicable? Whoever knew better how to enlighten and bring back souls that had withdrawn from God, or that wearied themselves in His service by an unreasonable fear?

"Happy then and useful inspiration [it was], to gather from his works the thoughts most fitted to enlighten pious and timorous souls, to console them, and to dilate their hearts dried up by fear! Father Huguet has given us, in this little work, the quintessence of everything that our amiable saint wrote most sweet and consoling, especially in his letters, in which that heart so good and tender, which God had formed to comfort the afflicted, is entirely revealed. The book is of the greatest assistance to the simple faithful, and to directors and confessors charged with comforting discouraged and troubled souls.

"A word now as to the method adopted. The author read, he tells us, with pen in hand, the works of the holy Bishop of Geneva; and, after noting the different passages which referred to the same subject, he arranged them in such order as to form a single chapter. A page is thus sometimes collected from seven or eight places in the saint's writings. Yet such is the connection of ideas that we scarcely perceive the labor, and everything seems to flow as from one fountainhead. As to the graceful, artless style of St. Francis de Sales, the author has lightly retouched it in some places, changing a few antiquated expressions that would be little intelligible nowadays. Without altering anything in substance, he has considered it a duty to suppress certain details and comparisons, whose want of simplicity, a common fault at present, might cloy the work. Everywhere we have the good shepherd, who, after the example of his Divine Master, instructs, cheers, and consoles, by the help of parables and similitudes, in the great art of using which perhaps he never had an equal.

"To add more clearness and authority to the book, the author has, from time to time, placed at the foot of the page some notes taken from the most esteemed writings of our greatest masters of the spiritual life, particularly Bossuet and Fenelon. These notes, happily selected, give a new value to the work. Should we now recommend it to all those whose souls have need to be encouraged and consoled—in a word, all the faithful?"

Introduction

By Père Huguet

"The writings of St. Francis de Sales are the fruit
of grace and experience."—Fenelon

THE great evil of our period is discouragement. Tempers and characters have become weak and degenerate.
Everyone agrees in saying that the most common obstacle, and the one most difficult to be overcome, which all those meet who labor for the conversion of sinners and the sanctification of pious souls, is want of confidence. The great evil that Jansenism wrought in the midst of us has not yet entirely disappeared: many still believe that perfection consists only in fearing the Lord and in trembling before Him, who, in His mercy, permits us to call Him *Our Father,* and to name Him *the good God.*

The generality of authors have placed in the *Lives of the Saints* an account of their heroic virtues only, without a single word of the defects and miseries which God left in them, in order to preserve them in humility and to

xvii

make them more indulgent towards their brethren; yet the history of their weaknesses would, according to the judicious remark of St. Francis de Sales, have done the greatest good to a large number of souls, who imagine that sanctity can, and should, be exempt, even in this world, from all alloy and all imperfection. It is to remedy, as far as lies in our power, these inconveniences, that we have gathered together, under appropriate headings, from the writings of the sweetest and most amiable of all the saints, those passages which are best calculated to enlighten pious souls, and to expand their hearts withered with fear.

The writings of St. Francis de Sales are admirably suited to times of trial and sadness. The soul enjoys in them an atmosphere of mild salubrity that strengthens and renews it. The doctrine there is holy and profound, under a most amiable exterior; the style adds, by its simple naïveté, to the charm of a clear and ingenuous fancy; we are instructed while we imagine ourselves distracted, and admire while we smile.

We hesitate not to say that no saint has ever contributed so much as St. Francis de Sales, by his immortal writings, to make piety loved and practiced in all classes of society.

"Under his pen," says the best of his biographers, "devotion is noble, true and rational; courtesy of manners, a spirit of sociality, all the charms of a well-ordered piety, form its cortege, if we may use the expression, and yet it is not disguised in order to appear the more agreeable. Everywhere the author's sweetness appears without weakness, and his firmness without bitterness. He teaches us to respect decorum, which he calls the gracefulness of virtue, to rise above nature without destroying it, to fly little by little towards Heaven like doves when we cannot soar thither like eagles, that is to say, to sanctify ourselves by ordinary means. There the mind contemplates truth, unveiled in majestic splendor, bedecked with maxims equally elegant and profound, clad in a style noble, flowing and natural, relieved by the justness of the expressions, sometimes fine and delicate, sometimes vivid and impressive, always graceful and varied: this is simplicity, with all the merit of beauty, for every idea is rendered by the proper word, and every word embellishes the thought. There, above all, the heart tastes an inexpressible pleasure; because the sweetness of the sentiment always seasons the precept, while the delicacy of the precaution that accompanies it secures its acceptance, and the artless candor and goodness of the author, who paints himself without intending it, make him beloved; at the same time the soul, embalmed in what it reads, deliciously participates in the sweetest and purest perfume of true piety."[1]

The style of St. Francis de Sales is a picture of his heart as much as of his mind: we feel that he loves and deserves to be loved, but that he wishes above all things that we should love God.

A special characteristic of St. Francis de Sales is that the frequent use he makes of figures and the comparisons which he endlessly multiplies, never weary. This style

---

1 *Life of St. Francis de Sales,* by M. the Curé of Saint Sulpice. This beautiful work has met with a success which surprises no one except its author, whose modesty and evangelical simplicity can alone equal his learning and his zeal for the conversion of souls.

would be clumsy in another author; with our saint it is a new pleasure, which draws away the reader and attracts him every moment, as a gentle magnet, and this with so much the more ease as the reader does not perceive it. One is led along unresistingly, yielding with pleasure to the charms of this enchanting style. An effect, so rare and wonderful, is owing not only to our saint's judicious choice of figures and comparisons, but also to his amiable character, to the sprightliness of his sentiments, and to the transports of his love for God, which burst forth even in the midst of the most abstract truths. He cannot contain the fire that consumes him; he allows it to escape by every sense. Moreover, he so well unites simplicity of diction with beauty of metaphor, that, in perusing his works, we feel the ornaments to flow from his pen without an effort on his part to seek them. A tender and compassionate soul, he is full of charity towards his friends. Let us hear him speak: "Through a great part of my soul I am poor and weak, but I have a boundless and almost immutable affection for those who favor me with their friendship. Whoever challenges me in the contest of friendship must be very determined, for I spare no effort. There is no person in the world who has a heart more tender and affectionate towards his friends than I, or one who feels a separation more acutely."

We have so often heard the following affecting words repeated, that they seem to have fallen from the mouth of the sweet Saviour Himself: "It has pleased God to make my heart thus. I wish to love this dear neighbor ever so much—ever so much I wish to love him! Oh, when shall we be all melted away in meekness and charity towards our neighbor! I have given him my whole person, my means, my affections, that they may serve him in all his wants."

This benignity, this gentleness, which breathed through the whole conduct of our saint, made St. Vincent de Paul exclaim with touching simplicity: "O my God! How good must Thou be, since the Bishop of Geneva is so good!"

It is in his works that he deposited the richest treasures of this sweet sensibility and of this playful imagination, which enabled him to lend to the driest subjects and the severest precepts of the evangelic law a charm that makes them loved even by the profane.

The French Academy proposed the writings of St. Francis de Sales as a model to all, even at a time when it extolled the faults of Corneille.

To make himself all to all, St. Francis de Sales descends to the level of the simple faithful, and there he loves to rest. Sometimes he places himself with his *Philothea* in the midst of the stormy sea of the world, and there casts out the anchor of faith; again, he takes his stand on the high road to show to the multitude, who pass indifferent and distracted along, the narrow way that leads to Heaven. We might say that he smoothes its roughness, so carefully does he conceal it under flowers. These are not deceitful flowers, by which virtue is disfigured in the endeavor to render it more attractive; they are those flowers of the soul which perfume without corrupting it, secret joys, interior consolations, ineffable delights, the anticipated inheritance of God's elect upon earth. The picture which he draws of devotion can only be compared to that of charity by

St. Paul. "In his writings," says Père de Tournemine, "we have the morality of the Sacred Scriptures and the Holy Fathers reduced to true principles and practical rules."

The doctrine of St. Francis de Sales is like a beautiful river which takes its rise in pure and elevated regions, and which, descending to the lowlands, spreads wide its banks, in order to reflect a broader expanse of Heaven; it is decked with the flowers of the prairie which it gathers on its course, and carries to the sea a tribute only of limpid and perfumed waters.

According to St. Francis de Sales, we must not be too punctilious in the practice of virtues, but approach them honestly, with liberty, in a *grosso modo* way. "Walk simply in the way of the Lord," he says, "and do not torment your mind. We must hate our defects, but with a tranquil and quiet hatred—not with a spiteful and troubled hatred— and, if necessary, have patience to witness them and to turn them to account by a holy self-abasement. For want of this, my daughter, your imperfections, which you view so closely, trouble you much, and by this means are retained, there being nothing that better preserves our defects than fretfulness and anxiety to remove them." (*Sermon for the Feast of St. Magdalen*).

He applies to himself what he counsels to others: "I know what sort of a being I am; yet even though I feel myself miserable, I am not troubled at it; nay, I am sometimes joyful at it, considering that I am a truly fit object for the mercy of God, to which I continually recommend you."

This devotion, at least in appearance so easy, naturally

pleases persons of the world, who, like the Count Bussy-Rabutin, say: "I merely wish to get into Heaven, and no higher." This nobleman, writing in another place, says: "Save us with our good Francis de Sales; he conducted people to Heaven by beautiful ways." Yet these beautiful ways were no other than the narrow way of which the Gospel speaks; only our amiable saint knew how to smooth its entrance and to hide its thorns under flowers.

St. Francis particularly excelled in comforting the afflicted and the sick; a few words falling from his heart sufficed to calm and enlighten them; his words entered into their soul as an oil of great sweetness, which moderated the heat of their malady. Let us hear him console a pious person to whom sickness was an insupportable burden: "Be not annoyed to remain in bed without meditation, for to endure the scourges of Our Lord is no less a good than to meditate. No, indeed; but it is much better to be on the cross with Jesus Christ, than merely to contemplate Him in prayer." To another, who was troubled at the sight of her miseries, he said: "When we happen to fall, let us cast down our heart before God, to say to Him, in a spirit of confidence and humility, 'Mercy, Lord! For I am weak.' Let us arise in peace, unite again the thread of our affections, and continue our work."

St. Francis de Sales was so much the better qualified to tranquilize and encourage souls inclined to diffidence and depression, as he had himself been obliged to pass through the severest trials, and arrived at the possession of peace of heart only by a total abandonment to God. "Since at every season of life, early or late, in youth or in old age, I can expect my salvation from the pure goodness and mercy of God alone, it is much better to cast myself from this moment into the arms of His clemency than to wait till another time. The greater part of the journey is over; let the Lord do with me according to His will; my fate is in His hands; let Him dispose of me according to His good pleasure."

The pious M. Olier, that great master of the spiritual life, very much esteemed St. Francis de Sales. "God," he says, "wishing to raise him up as a torch in the midst of His Church to enlighten an immense number, replenished him with the most marvelous gifts of understanding, knowledge, and wisdom, proportioned to His designs. As for his knowledge, it was evidently more than human, and the effect of the Divine Spirit."

If you wish to know Francis de Sales thoroughly, to be initiated into the most secret mysteries of that vast understanding and that perfect heart, read and re-read his *Letters,* in which every subject, from the most humble to the most sublime, from a simple how-do-you-do to a description of ecstasies and eternal beatitudes, is treated of in the style that best suits it. Read, above all, the *Letters to Madame de Chantal,* and those which treat of the *direction of souls.* Considering these admirable letters, Bossuet says: "Francis de Sales is truly sublime; there is no one among moderns with such sweetness, who has a hand so steady and experienced as his, to elevate souls to perfection and to detach them from themselves." The letter written after the death of his mother is of a primitive simplicity, and a sublime model of Christian resignation; we imagine that we hear

St. Augustine weeping over St. Monica, and the tears it makes us shed have nothing of bitterness, so sweet is the death of the just when thus related.

The learned and pious Archbishop of Cambray continually recommended the perusal of our saint's writings. "You cannot read anything more useful," says Fenelon, "than the books of St. Francis de Sales; everything there is consoling and pleasing, though he does not say a word but to help us to die. His artless style displays an amiable simplicity, which is above all, the flourishes of the profane writer. You see a man who, with great penetration and a perfect clearness of mind to judge of the reality of things, and to know the human heart, desires only to speak as a good-natured friend, to console, to solace, to enlighten, to perfect his neighbor. No person was better acquainted than he with the highest perfection; but he repeated himself for the little, and never disdained anything, however small. He made himself all to all, not to please all, but to gain all, and to gain them to Jesus Christ, not to himself."

To this judgment of the pious Bishop of Cambray we shall add that of the learned Bourdaloue: "The doctrine of St. Francis de Sales is a food, not of earth, but of Heaven, which, from the same substance, nourishes, like the manna, all kinds of persons; and I am able to say, without offending against the respect which I owe to all other writers, that after the Holy Scriptures there are no works that have better maintained piety among the faithful than those of this holy bishop."

The illustrious Monsignore of Paris shared the same

xxvi   CONSOLING THOUGHTS OF ST. FRANCIS DE SALES

sentiments. "All that can contribute," he says, "to make the most amiable of saints better known to the world must be useful to the cause of our holy religion."

Thus, the three men who were the glory of the clergy of France in the age of Louis XIV were unanimous in esteeming and praising the works of this great master of the spiritual life.

Protestants themselves are obliged to render justice to the exceptional merit of the works of St. Francis de Sales. One of their best authors[2] thus appreciates the writings of the blessed Bishop of Geneva: "From its first appearance, the *Introduction to a Devout Life* had a universal success in France, and editions succeeded one another rapidly. This was an event of great consequence in regard to such a book, and Catholicism could most justly rejoice at it. The learned controversies of Bellarmine had been of far less advantage: they had indeed fitted for theological discussion a clergy who found themselves face to face with superior forces; but from the first blow, the *Introduction* could make conquests to a religion whose practices were presented under forms so amiable, and even so delightful. . . . Among Calvinistic gentlemen solicited to abjure their faith, the little book served as an occasion for more than one renunciation. In this respect, the *Introduction to a Devout Life* was, in the beginning of the century, what the *Exposition of the Catholic Faith* was in the middle, and had effects quite similar. Of all that St. Francis de Sales has written, his *Letters* are the most widely spread: Protestants read them after a

---

2   *History of French Literature*, by M. Sayous.

selection, for all would not suit their taste; but in each class, the amiable and glowing piety, the grace—what shall I say? The wit, the familiar gossip, with which the Bishop allows his pen to twirl along, have a singular charm; and never does the afflicted or dejected heart disdain the consolation and encouragement which it finds in perusing them."

It is in his correspondence that we must study the great, the holy Bishop of Geneva; there we shall find humility unparalleled, a joyous cordiality, peace unutterable, the sole desire of accomplishing the will of God.

There we shall find that elegance, ever new, in thought and in expression; that richness of beautiful images and of fine comparisons borrowed from things most familiar: the rose, the pigeon, the halcyon, the bee, the odorous plants of Arabia; that dovelike simplicity, that childlike candor which does not, however, exclude, on due occasions, a manly strength and energy; that chaste tenderness which could only come from Heaven; that gentle meekness which holds the key of every heart.

We shall be the less surprised at the eulogies given to the writings of St. Francis de Sales by the most experienced doctors and the most eminent personages, when we consider with what maturity and wisdom they were composed. Those beautiful pages, which seem to flow as from a well, so free and natural are the doctrine and the style, are the fruit of the most serious study and the most assiduous meditation, joined with a great knowledge of the human heart, which he had acquired in the direction of souls.[3]

---

3 *Spirit of St. Francis de Sales.*

His beautiful *Treatise on the Love of God* is the result of twenty-four years' preaching, according to the statement of the author himself, and the fruit of such profound study, that there are fourteen lines in it, which, as he told Mgr. Camus, Bishop of Belley, had cost him the reading of more than twelve hundred pages in folio.[4] After this, we should not be surprised at the unexampled success which has crowned the writings of St. Francis de Sales. The *Treatise on the Love of God* is a most beautiful book, and one that has had a great circulation. All the agitations, all the inconsistencies of the human heart are painted in it with inimitable art. We behold there the exercises of love, contemplation, the repose of the soul in God, its languors, its transports, its dereliction, its dying sadness, its return to courage, the abandonment of the docile spirit to the secret ways of Providence. When the *Introduction to a Devout Life* appeared in the world, it created an extraordinary sensation; everyone wished to procure it, to read it, and, having read it, to read it again. Very soon it was translated into nearly all the languages of Europe, and editions succeeded one another so rapidly that in 1656 it had reached the fortieth. Henry IV, on reading it, declared that the work far surpassed his expectations; Mary of Medici, his wife, sent it bound in diamonds and precious stones to James, King of England; and this monarch, one of the most learned who ever occupied a throne, conceived such an esteem for it, that, notwithstanding his schismatical and spiteful preju-

---

4   It is related that the publisher, in gratitude for the considerable gain he had derived from the sale of the *Introduction to a Devout Life*, made a journey to Annecy expressly to offer as a gift to the author a sum of four hundred crowns of gold. *(Memoirs of the Academic Society of Savoy,* Vol. II).

dices against Catholic writers, he carried it always about
with him and often read it. Many times he was heard to
say: "Oh, how I should wish to know the author! He is
certainly a great man, and among all our bishops there is
not one capable of writing in this manner, which breathes
of Heaven and the angels." The general of the Feuillants,
speaking of this work, calls it the most perfect book that
mortal hand ever composed, a book that one would always
wish to read again after having read it many times, and
he adds this beautiful eulogium, that in reading it he who
would not be a Christian should become better, and he
who would be better should become perfect.[5]

The Church, directed by the Holy Spirit, exhorts all
her children to be guided by the counsels of St. Francis de
Sales. *Admonished by his directions,* she says in his Office.
She assures us that his works have diffused a bright light
amongst the faithful, to whom they point out a way as sure
as it is easy, to arrive at perfection.

We could, if our design permitted it, multiply evidence
in favor of the works of St. Francis de Sales. We shall ter-
minate this introduction by some extracts from a letter of
Pope Alexander VII, one of the greatest of his panegyrists:
"I conjure you anew to make the works of M. de Sales your
delight and your dearest study. I have read them I cannot
tell how many times, and I would not dispense myself from
reading them again; they never lose the charm of novelty;
they always seem to me to say something more than they
had said before. If you trust me, these writings should be

---

5 *Life of St. Francis de Sales,* by M. the Abbé Hamon.

the mirror of your life, and the rule by which to form your every action and your every thought. As for me, I confess to you that from often reading them I have become like a repository of his most beautiful sentiments and the principal points of his doctrine, that I ruminate over them at my leisure, that I taste them, and that I make them, so to speak, pass into my very blood and substance. Such is my opinion of this great saint, exhorting you with all my heart to follow him."

If in gathering these lovely flowers and binding them into bunches, we have lessened their beauty or their perfume, we trust that still they will at least a little serve those severely tried souls for whom we intend them; we shall consider it an ample recompense for all our trouble, if, even in a single heart, they increase confidence in God, and the desire to love and serve Him generously.

"Most holy Mother of God, the most lovable, the most loving, and the most loved, of creatures! Prostrate at thy feet, I dedicate and consecrate to thee this little work of love, in honor of the immense greatness of thy love. O Jesus! To whom could I more fitly offer these words of Thy love than to the most amiable heart of the well-beloved of Thy soul?"[6]

6   Dedication of the *Treatise on the Love of God,* by St. Francis de Sales.

—THIRD BOOK—

Consoling Thoughts on Sickness and Death

_____

CHAPTER ONE

THE TIME OF SICKNESS

WHEN sick, offer all your sorrows, your languors, and your pains to the Lord, and beg of Him to unite them with the torments which He endured for you. Obey the doctor; take medicine, food, and other remedies, for the love of God, remembering the gall which He took for the love of you; desire to be cured in order to serve Him; do not refuse to languish in order to obey Him; and dispose yourself to die, if He wishes it to be so, in order to praise and enjoy Him. Remember that bees, during the time in which they make honey, live on a very bitter kind of nourishment, and that in like manner we can never more properly elicit the great acts of meekness and patience, or better compose the honey of excellent virtues, than when we eat the bitter bread of tribulation and live in the midst of anguish. And as that honey which is made from the flowers of thyme, a small but bitter herb, is the best of all, so that

3

virtue which is formed in the bitterness of pain and humiliation is the most excellent of all. Tribulation and sickness are well calculated to advance us in virtue, on account of the many resignations which they oblige us to make into the hands of Our Lord.[1]

Your body is weak; but charity, which is the nuptial robe, covers it.[2] A weak person excites all those who know him to a holy support, and gives them even a particular tenderness for him, provided he shows that he carries his cross lovingly and devoutly.

We must be equally free to take and ask for remedies, as sweet and courageous to support our illness. He who can preserve meekness in the midst of sorrows and sufferings, and peace in the midst of bustle and business, is almost perfect; and though there are few persons found, even in religion, who have attained to this degree of happiness, yet there are some, and there have been some in all times, and it is to this highest point we should aspire.

The life of a person in good health is almost entirely barren, and that of one in sickness may be a continual harvest; we must accommodate ourselves to necessity, and turn all to our eternal happiness. Ah, how little it matters if everything dies in us, provided that God reigns and lives there! Evils often happen to us in order that, not having

---

1 Sickness separates the Christian from the world and from all inebriation of the senses; it causes silence around him; it changes his body, which is the usual instrument of his illusions and vain desires, into an altar of sacrifice and expiation; the conversation of men is no longer sought for; everything tells him to look inwards, and the Christian sufferer naturally finds himself alone with God.

2 "The nuptial robe" is Sanctifying Grace. The virtue of charity accompanies Sanctifying Grace, and theologians sometimes refer to the state of grace as "the state of charity."—*Publisher, 2013.*

done much penance voluntarily for our sins, we do some unavoidably. Let us, nevertheless, use suitable remedies, but with such resignation that if the divine hand render them unavailing, we may acquiesce in its arrangement, and if it render them efficacious, we may bless it for its mercy. Oh! How little it were, though all the hours of our life were sad and full of affliction, provided that the hour of our death shall be happy and bring us true consolation! Ought we not to wish as much to live on Mount Calvary as on Mount Thabor? It is good to be with Our Lord, wherever He is, on the cross as well as in glory. The hand of God is equally amiable, when it dispenses afflictions and when it distributes consolations. We must not say a word against the decrees of the celestial will, which disposes of its own in accordance with its greater glory. It is not in our power to retain the consolations which God bestows upon us, unless the one of loving Him above all things, which is a favor supremely desirable. O God, how good a thing it is to live only in God, to labor only in God, and to rejoice only in God!

It is on this account that we must have patience not only to be sick, but to have the sickness God wishes, in the place where He wishes, among the persons whom He wishes, obeying the physician in each and every thing (except as regards ejaculatory prayers, which he cannot and should not prohibit, if they be not too frequent), taking medicines, meats, and other remedies, for the love of God, remembering the gall which Our Lord took for the love of us, desiring to be cured in order to serve Him, not refusing to suffer in order to obey Him, and disposing ourselves to die, if He should so will it, in order to praise and enjoy Him.

Lord Jesus, what true happiness has a soul dedicated to God, in being well exercised in tribulations, before quitting this life!

How can we know a sincere and fervent love, unless we see it in the midst of thorns and crosses, and particularly when it is left among them for a long time?

Thus our dear Saviour testified His immeasurable love, by the measure of His labors and His Passion.

Manifest your love for the Spouse of your heart on the bed of sorrow; it was on the bed of sorrow that He formed your heart, even before it was formed in the world, beholding it as yet only in His divine designs.

Alas! Our Saviour counted all your sorrows, all your sufferings, and purchased, at the price of His blood, the patience and the love that were necessary for you, in order to worthily refer your pains to His glory and your own salvation.

Be consoled in the thought that God sends you these crosses; for nothing comes from His divine hand but what is for the benefit of souls that fear Him, either to purify them or to confirm them in His holy love.[3]

---

3   "The remembrance which the saints in Heaven have of their sufferings and humiliations, delights them; they celebrate them in their songs of gladness, and if they could have any regret, it would be that they had not suffered more. The saints who reign in Heaven have taught these things to persons who are not there yet. Let us endeavor to remember this holy doctrine; it is understood *by the saints.*

"The great characteristic of sanctity is love of suffering, as its peculiar seal is spiritual joy; one produces the other. This is a mystery; but strive sincerely to enter into it, and you will find that I have reason for what I say.

"Let us not speak ill of the cross; it has been sent to us to warn us, to detach us from the earth, to conduct us to our end. Let us leave it only to cast ourselves into God. We have much need of suffering . . . let us suffer well!"—*P. De Ravignan.*

Pains considered in themselves cannot be loved, but considered in their source, that is to say, in the divine will which appoints them, they are infinitely amiable. Behold the rod of Moses on the ground, it is a frightful serpent; see it in the hand of Moses, it is a wand of wonders. Behold tribulations in themselves, they are terrors; regard them in the will of God, they are delights.

You will be truly happy, if, with a heart filially loving, you receive that which Our Lord sends you from a heart paternally careful of your perfection.

Look often to the length of eternity, and you will not be troubled at the accidents of this mortal life.

If you have scarcely any gold or frankincense to offer to Our Lord, you have at least some myrrh, and I am sure He will accept it most willingly, for this fruit of life wished to be committed to the myrrh of bitterness, both at His birth and at His death.

Jesus glorified is beautiful; but although He is always infinitely good, He seems to be yet more beautiful when crucified. Thus He wishes to be your spouse at present; in the future you will have Him glorified.

On what occasions can we make great acts of the union of our heart with the will of God, of the mortification of our self-love, and of the love of our own abjection, if not on these?

God wishes thus to exercise our heart. It is not severity, it is clemency. Let not our will, but His most holy will, be done.

Let us have good courage, for, provided that our heart is faithful to Him, He will not load us above our strength, and He will carry our burden with us, when He sees that with a good affection we bow down our shoulders beneath it.

I desire your advancement in solid piety, and this advancement has its difficulties, given to train you in the school of the cross, in which alone our souls can be perfected.

Be assured that my heart expects the day of your consolation with as much ardor as your own; but wait—*wait,* I say, *while waiting,* to use the words of the Holy Scripture. Now, to wait while waiting means not to be disquieted while waiting; for there are many who, while waiting, do not wait, but are troubled and uneasy.

It is not with spiritual rose bushes as with material ones; on the latter the thorns remain and the roses pass away, on the former the thorns pass away and the roses remain.

It is a great error to imagine that the services we render to God, without relish, without tenderness of heart, are little agreeable to Him, since, on the contrary, our actions are just like roses, which, while fresh, have more beauty; being, nevertheless, dry, they have more perfume and strength. In the very same manner, while our works performed with tenderness of heart are more agreeable to us—to us, I say, who desire only our own pleasure; yet, being done in aridity, they have more excellence and merit before God.

For to love God in sugar, little children could nearly do as much; but to love Him in senna, that is the proof of a loving fidelity.

To say: "Live Jesus on Thabor!" St. Peter, rough as he

was, had enough courage; but to say: Live Jesus on Calvary! That belonged only to the Mother, and the beloved disciple who was left to her as a child.

Oh! How blessed, my dear souls, will all those be who will not be scandalized at the opprobriums and ignominies of Our Lord, and who, during this life, will be crucified with Him, meditating on His Passion, carrying His mortification about with them, and not being ashamed to see that He was the scorn, the refuse, and the outcast of the world![4]

Beyond a doubt, if we wish to be saved, we must attach ourselves to the cross of our Saviour, meditate on it, and carry about His mortification in our bodies: there is no other way to Heaven; Our Lord passed by it first. [You may experience] As many ecstasies, elevations of soul, and raptures as you please; ascend, if you can, even to the third heaven with St. Paul; but still, if you do not remain on the cross of Our Lord and exercise yourself in mortification, I tell you that all the rest is vanity, and that you will remain void of every good, without virtue, and liable to be scandalized with the Jews at the Passion of our divine Saviour. In fine, there is no other gate by which to enter into Heaven than that of humiliation and mortification.

---

4 "The same God sanctified both Thabor and Calvary, to make us understand the mysterious union that exists between ignominy and glory: they ought to be the same to us. We should remember that in consolation or in temptation, God is ever the same Being in our regard; He is always a Saviour, always great, always powerful, always turned toward us with infinite love. Let us then say on every occasion: God is always the same, this thought suffices for me, I wait for Him. . . . If Jesus shows His glory and splendor to His Apostles, it is to lead them afterward to the cross, it is to prepare them for sacrifice and immolation. In undertaking the labor of sanctification, we must always say: The joy of Thabor may be given sometimes on earth, but only for a very short and almost indiscernible time. Pain is what is regularly given us, to establish us in devotedness and zeal."—*P. De Ravignan.*

CHAPTER TWO

SPIRITUAL ADVANCEMENT IN SICKNESS[1]

B UT, you say, you can scarcely fix your mind on the fatigues which Our Lord endured for you, so long as your sorrows press upon you. Very well! It is not necessary that you should do so, but only that, as frequently as you can, you should lift up your heart to our Saviour, making some acts like the following:

1. Accepting this sorrow from His hand, as if you saw Him actually laying it upon your head.

2. Offering yourself to suffer still more.

3. Conjuring Him, by the merit of His torments,

---

1 "When everything in the world smiles on us, we easily attach ourselves to it: the enchantment is too powerful and the attraction too strong. If God loves us, be assured that He will not allow us to repose at our ease in this land of exile. He disturbs us in our vain amusements, He interrupts the course of our imaginary felicity, lest we should be carried away by the rivers of Babylon, that is to say, by the current of transitory pleasures. Believe, then, O children of the new alliance! That when God sends you afflictions, He wishes to break the bonds which attach you to the world and to recall you to your true country."—*Bossuet*.

to accept these little inconveniences which you endure in union with the pains which He suffered on the cross.

4. Declaring that you wish not only to suffer, but to love and caress these evils, being sent from so good and so kind a father.

5. Invoking the martyrs and the many holy men and women who now enjoy Heaven for having been afflicted on earth.

There are many persons who, when sick or afflicted in any manner whatever, take care not to complain, or to act delicately, because they think with reason that this would be a weakness and an immortification; yet at the same time they earnestly desire and act in such a manner that everyone should pity them, that everyone should compassionate their lot, that everyone should look upon them as not only afflicted, but also patient and courageous. Now, I acknowledge there is patience in this, but it is a false patience, which, in fact, is no other thing than a most refined pretense and subtle vanity. "They have glory," says the Apostle, "but not in the eyes of God." The true patient does not complain of his sickness, or desire to be pitied; he speaks of it sincerely, truthfully, and simply, without bewailing himself, without being angry, without making his malady appear worse than it is. And if he is pitied, he suffers patiently to be pitied, unless he is pitied for something which he does not suffer; for then he modestly declares he does not suffer that, and remains thus peacefully between truth and patience, telling his sickness and not complaining of it.

There is no harm in desiring a remedy; on the contrary, we should carefully endeavor to procure it; for God, who sends you sickness, is also the author of remedies.

Nevertheless, you must employ those remedies with such resignation that if His Divine Majesty wishes the sickness to overcome them, you may acquiesce therein, and if He wishes the remedies to overcome the disease, you may bless Him.[2]

My God, how happy you are, if you continue thus under the hand of God, humbly, sweetly, and unaffectedly!

Ah! I hope that this pain in your head will much benefit your heart. It is now more than ever, and on the best assurance, you can show to our sweet Saviour that with all your affliction you said and say: "Live Jesus!"

Live Jesus, and may He reign in the midst of our sorrows, since we cannot reign or live but by those of His death!

Hope then always in Him; and to hope in Him, belong always to Him. Often immolate your heart to His love, even on the altar of the cross, on which He immolated His for the love of you. The cross is the royal gate by which we enter into the temple of sanctity.

If envy could reign in the kingdom of eternal love, the angels would envy two prerogatives in man: one is that Our Lord endured the cross for us, and not for them, at least

---

2   "As to the motives you may take for the preservation of your health, besides that of obedience, which delivers you from all self-seeking, you ought to consider your body as the temple of the Holy Ghost, who has made you its guardian, and that, as it is not your own, you must render an account of it to its Master. You ought to do the same for it, as if you were responsible for a chapel which was falling to ruin, and which you were obliged to repair. Moreover, your body is a member of Jesus Christ; be careful then of it, as if Our Lord would complain of the ill treatment He had received from you. Treat it, again, like that of a third person, to whom you would render a charity. And, in fine, remember that, as a child of God the Father, you belong to His family, and He wishes your body to be taken care of, and to be kept up. It belongs to Him, He has purchased it with the blood of His Son, He has a right over it, and He wishes us to preserve it, that we may employ it in His service."—*M. Olier.*

not so entirely; the other, that men endure something for Our Lord: the suffering of God for man, and the suffering of man for God.[3]

Remembering the cross you carry, I say to you: Love your cross well, for it is all of gold if you regard it with eyes of love; and while, on the one side, you behold the love of your heart dead and crucified amid nails and thorns, you will find, on the other, an assemblage of precious pearls to compose the crown of glory which awaits you, if, while awaiting it, you lovingly carry the crown of thorns with your King, who so much desired to suffer before entering into His felicity.[4]

Let our dear Jesus crucified then rest forever as a bouquet on your bosom; yes, for His nails are more desirable than carnations, and His thorns than roses. My God, how I desire that you should be holy, and all odoriferous with the perfumes of the Saviour!

---

3   Perfection does not consist in consolation, but in the submission of our will to God, especially in times of bitterness. Let us bear in mind that the obedience of Jesus Christ became perfect when His tongue and His mouth were burning, and when His cruel thirst was increased by vinegar and gall; we ought to value more the aridity and desolation of a submissive soul than the loving languor and delicious sweetness of an overflowing devotion.

4   St. John Damascene teaches us that the Son of God deified all the goods of this life by His Incarnation, and all its evils by His Passion; that, in a manner, He united them hypostatically to His Divinity; so that, as we adore what touched the body of Jesus Christ, we should adore evils of every kind, because they have entered into His heart; there is not one of them which did not touch His sacred body, or was not embraced by the desires of His holy soul. This was St. Anselm's thought when he said that *he adored all the evils of this life as so many sacraments.* The Sacraments produce grace in those who receive them worthily; so the cross sanctifies those who touch it; and as the Son of God is always present in the Sacrament of the Eucharist, so we can say with truth that He is found present in our afflictions. Hence that burning expression of faith and love in the mouth of a holy religious, prostrate at the feet of a sick man: *I adore Jesus Christ in this suffering body; my faith shows Him to me in a manner less real, but more sensible than in the consecrated Host. I see Him present, not only as a physician is with his patient, a father with his son, a friend with his friend, but as the soul is with the body, the head with its members.*

The *Our Father* which you say for the headache is not forbidden; but, my God! No, I would not have courage to ask Our Lord, by the pain He had in His head, that I might not have any pains in mine. Ah! Did He suffer, that we might not suffer? St. Catherine of Siena seeing that her Saviour presented her with two crowns, one of gold, the other of thorns: "Oh, I wish for the crown of sorrow," said she, "in this world; the other will do for Heaven!" I would desire to employ the crowning of Our Lord to obtain a crown of patience around my headache.

Live entirely among the thorns of the Saviour's crown, and say continually: Live Jesus! Our flesh is very delicate in not desiring anything unpleasant, but still the repugnances which you feel do not show a want of love. For, as I think, if we believed that by being flayed alive, He would love us more, we would have ourselves flayed alive, not indeed without repugnance, but in spite of repugnance.

Do not say that you would wish to recover your health in order the better to love and serve God; for, on the contrary, it would be only the better to serve your own contentment, which you would prefer to the contentment of God. The will of God is as good in sickness as it is in health, and is usually better. And if we love health better, let us not say it is the better to serve God; for who does not see that it is health we seek in the will of God, and not the will of God in health?

Poor and contemptible creatures that we are, we can hardly do anything good in this miserable life, except to endure some adversity. We seldom do God a service on one side, but we undo it on another. If by an action we desire to unite ourselves to Him, we often separate ourselves from Him by the evil circumstances which accompany it. On this account, it is good to quit Him in sweetness to serve Him humbly in bitterness.

We must act with Our Lord by serving Him faithfully so long as health is good, and suffer with Him by patient endurance, when He sends us sorrows and afflictions.

Judge now, Theotime, whether you should regret the time you spend under the pressure of suffering, since in each one of those moments you may earn an eternal crown. How many crowns in an hour! How many in a day! How many in a year! Oh, what treasures! What glory for Heaven! "I would prefer one of those days," says a holy religious, "to all the exploits of conquerors." When we think on eternity, where there will be nothing more to suffer, where we can give nothing more to God, and where God will have nothing more to do but to load us with His gifts, all the miseries of this life appear infinitely amiable, and there is not a moment which ought not to be a moment of the cross or of humiliation. How precious then is the time of this life, and holy is its use, when joined with pain and bitterness!

The heart united to the heart of God cannot refrain from loving Him, or from accepting willingly the arrows which the hand of God shoots at it. St. Blandina found no greater relief amid the wounds of her martyrdom than the sacred thought which she expressed in these few words: "I am a Christian." Blessed is the heart that knows how to breathe this sigh!

The only cure for the most of our maladies and infirmities, whether corporal or spiritual, is patience and conformity to the Divine Will, resigning ourselves to the good pleasure of God, without reserve or exception, in health, in sickness, in contempt, in honor, in consolation, in desolation, in time, and in eternity; willingly accepting pains of mind and body from His most amiable hand, as if we saw it present; offering ourselves to endure even more, should it appear good to Him. No one can tell how pure and meritorious such an acceptance of the will of God renders our sufferings, when, with meekness, patience, and love, we receive the afflictions which we must endure, in consideration of the eternity during which God has willed them, and because they are now conformable to His Providence. As soon as the divine good pleasure appears, we should immediately range ourselves on its side.

You are aware that the fire which Moses saw in the desert was a figure of holy love, and that, as its flames were nourished in the midst of thorns, so the exercises of sacred love are performed much better in the midst of tribulation than in the midst of comfort.[5]

You have then good reason to know that Our Lord desires you to profit by His love, since He sends you such

---

5 "What can the soldier hope for, whose captain disdains to prove him? But, on the other hand, if the soldier is exercised in a variety of laborious undertakings, he has reason to expect promotion. O delicate piety, which never tasted afflictions, piety nurtured in the shade and repose! I hear thee discourse of the future life; thou pretendest to the crown of immortality, but thou shouldst not reverse the order of the Apostle: 'Patience produces trial, and trial, hope.' If then thou expectest the glory of God, come, that I may put thee to the test which God has proposed for His servants. Here is a disaster, a loss of goods, a contradiction, a sickness; what! Thou beginnest to murmur, O poor disconcerted piety! Thou canst not endure it, O piety without strength or foundation! Ah, thou didst never deserve the name of Christian piety, thou wast only a vain phantom; thou didst glitter like gold in the sun, but thou couldst not bear the fire of the crucible; thou mayest deceive men by a false appearance, but thou art not worthy of God, or of the purity of the future kingdom."—*Bossuet.*

health as is always uncertain, and many other trials. My God! How sweet a thing it is to see Our Lord crowned with thorns on the cross and with glory in Heaven! For this encourages us to receive contradictions lovingly, knowing well that by the crown of thorns we shall arrive at the crown of felicity. Keep yourself ever closely attached to Our Lord, and you will meet with no evil that will not be converted into good.

Often look with the interior eyes of your soul on Jesus Christ crucified, naked, blasphemed, calumniated, abandoned, overwhelmed with every kind of weariness, disgust, and sadness; and consider that all your sorrows are not at all comparable to His, either in kind or in degree, and that you will never suffer anything approaching to that which He has suffered for you.

Consider the pains which the martyrs endured formerly, and those which so many persons endure even at this day, greater beyond all proportion than any which afflict you, and say: "Alas! My labors are consolations, and my pains are roses, if I compare myself with those who, without resource, without sympathy, without any alleviation, live in a continual death, overwhelmed with afflictions, a thousand times greater than mine."

We do not think of death; and you, being in health, are obliged to think no longer of life. We avoid the cross of Jesus Christ; and He Himself nails you to it. We do not wish to feel the efficacy of sufferings, for we desire to be virtuous without patience; and Our Lord, who loves you more than you can love yourself, applies Himself till He is tired to purify you, while perhaps He leaves others to themselves.

Oh, how happy you are to have something to suffer for Our Lord, who, having founded the Church Militant and Triumphant on the cross, always favors those who carry the cross! Since you cannot remain very long in this world, it is well that the little time you do spend in it should be employed in suffering.

If I had anything to desire, it would be that my death should be preceded by a long illness; for, by this means, the affection of my friends would relent, and they would no longer have so much care of visiting me. The diligence, in like manner, of my servants would gradually diminish, and everyone would receive comfort by my death.

Chapter Three

Prayers Suitable to the Sick[1]

THE bed of the sick is an altar of sacrifice. . . . Happy is the just man who disturbs not the sacrifice by his murmurs and his cries, who adores the beneficent hand

---

1 "Be not troubled about the indisposition which the will of God has allowed to come upon me. It is a special order of His goodness and His providence, for which we ought to thank Him. There are many things in me to be purified, and sickness is the best means for doing so; He has usually treated me after this manner, of His infinite goodness. May He be forever praised! I cannot in my infirmities apply myself to prayer so assiduously as I thought to do when retiring from the din of the city; but the sacrifice of our body, of our mind, of our time, and of all that we have, must serve as a substitute. The ill use I have made of my health is the cause of my infirmities; but may God be pleased of His goodness to satisfy Himself in us as He desires, and to content Himself, should it so please Him, in our destruction and in our consummation! All these evils are only shadows in comparison with what our sins deserve. What mercy and goodness of God, to make us perform so sweet a penance! Far from complaining, let us adore our Saviour's love, which treats us with so much clemency, and which deigns, as St. Paul says, to complete that which was wanting to His sufferings. It seems to me an incomparable honor Our Lord does us, in using our bodies to suffer again in them for the glory of His Father. Let us, then, with the Apostle, glory in our infirmities, that the divine power may dwell in us; pay great attention to the sentiments which Our Lord will give you during the holy time of your infirmity; for it is the ordinary method of God to accomplish in sickness that which, if we may so speak, He could not well accomplish in health. Above all, abandon yourself entirely to Him, to do what He wishes with you, resigning yourself as a victim to suffer everything, and even the death which your sins deserve."—*M. Olier.*

that is hidden under the instruments which it vouchsafes to employ, who blesses the salutary strokes, who feels the honor of the distinction! How brilliant will his soul depart from the crucible of tribulations! It is as gold tried seven times, it is marked with the seal of the elect, it bears the impress of Jesus Christ.

It is not good to require Mass in bedrooms; from your bed adore Our Lord on the altar, and be content. Daniel, being unable to go to the Temple, turned towards it; do you the same. But I am of opinion that you should communicate[2] every Sunday and great feasts on your bed, so long as the doctor permits it. Our Lord will willingly visit you on the bed of affliction.

My dear daughter, if you cannot make long prayers during your infirmities, and during the infirmities of your husband, make your infirmity itself a prayer, by offering it to Him who so much loved our infirmities, that on the day of His espousals and of the joy of His heart, as the inspired lover terms it, He was crowned with them and gloried in them.

Aspire often to God by short but burning elevations of the heart; admire His beauty, invoke His aid, adore His goodness, give Him your soul a thousand times a day, fix your eyes interiorly on His abode, and stretch out your hand to Him, as a little child towards its father, that He may conduct you.

This exercise is not difficult, for it may be intertwined with all our affairs and occupations, without encumbering or delaying them. The traveler who takes a little wine to

---

2   Communicate—that is, receive Holy Communion.—*Publisher*, 2013.

cheer his heart, though he stops a short while on the way, does not interrupt his journey, but rather acquires new strength to accomplish it more quickly, only waiting to advance the better.

When did Our Lord render most glory to God, if not when, laid upon the cross, His hands and feet were pierced? This was the greatest act of His service. And what use did He make of those moments? To suffer, to offer; His sufferings were an oblation, an odor of sweetness, to His Father. While you are sick you must lay aside a regular meditation; but to endure the scourges of Our Lord is no less a good than to meditate; no, indeed, but it is rather better to be on the cross with Jesus Christ than merely to contemplate Him in prayer.[3]

Manage yourself very cautiously, so long as your present infirmity continues; be not at all uneasy to force yourself to any kind of exercise, unless gently. If you be tired on your knees, sit up. If you have not attention to pray for half an hour, pray for a quarter, or for only half a quarter. I beg of you to place yourself in the presence of God, and to suffer your sorrows before Him.

As for meditation, the doctors have reason: while you are so unwell, you must give it up, but to supply its place, you must double your ejaculatory prayers, and refer

---

3 "When some sickness or engagement prevents us from making prayer, we must hope that an hour of suffering will be as agreeable in the eyes of God as an hour of prayer, during which we might, perhaps, seek to gratify ourselves. When we imagine that the multiplicity and perplexity of our exterior occupations hinder us from spending some time with God, or thinking often of Him, let us remember that it is not the repose of nature, but that of grace which is necessary for the soul in order to attend to God; this repose is found in the cross, in pain, in the love of contempt, better than anywhere else."—*The Interior Christian.*

everything to God by a simple acquiescence in His good
pleasure, which will not by any means separate you from
Him, while preventing you from meditation, but will unite
you more closely to Him by the exercise of a holy and tranquil resignation.[4]

What matters it how we belong to God, in one manner or in another? Truly, since we seek Him alone, and since
we find Him no less in mortification than in prayer, especially when He touches us with sickness, one mode ought
to be as good to us as another; besides, the ejaculations and
aspirations of our soul are true and continual prayers, and
the suffering of evil is the most worthy offering that we can
make to Him who has saved us by suffering. Read a good
book from time to time, for it also supplies the place of
meditation.[5]

Disquiet not yourself about being unable to serve God
according to your taste; for, by accommodating yourself
well to inconveniences, you will serve Him according to
His taste, which is better than yours. May He be forever
praised and glorified![6]

---

4 "Your life has been entirely consecrated to piety by exercises which are, as it were,
the food of your soul; but a sickness breaks the chain of pious practices you had
imposed on yourself. Already, you can no longer assist at Mass, even on Sunday; you
are deprived of the sacred banquet of Communion; very soon, your state of weakness
will prohibit you from prayer. Pious soul! Do not complain: you are called to the
honor of nourishing your soul by participating with Jesus Christ *in a meat of which,*
perhaps, *you did not know,* but the use of which will make your sickness a powerful
means of sanctification. *My meat,* He said to His disciples, *is to do the will of Him
who sent me.* This is the meat that is presented to you, and by it alone can we live to
eternal life. Prayer itself is inefficacious, if not vivified by this salutary nourishment,
according to the words of our Saviour in the Holy Gospel: *Not they who say to me,
Lord! Lord! Shall enter into the kingdom of heaven; but he who does the will of my Father
shall enter into it."—Providence.*
5 The *Treatise on Conformity to the Will of God,* by Rodriguez; the *Comforter of the Sick,*
by P. Lambilotte; the *Sufferings of Christ,* by Father Thomas.
6 "You are aware that it is God who has reduced you to your present state; it is He then

When God will have restored your health, you must resume your prayer, at least for half an hour in the morning, and a quarter of an hour in the evening before supper; for, when once Our Lord has given you a relish for this heavenly honey, it would be a great reproach in you to disrelish it. You must then take courage, and not allow conversation to deprive you of so rich a treat as is that of speaking heart to heart with your God.

Do not refrain when you desire to complain; but I would wish this to be done to God with a filial spirit, as a tender child does to its mother; for, provided it be done lovingly, there is no danger in complaining, or in asking a cure, or in changing place, or in being comforted; only do it with love and resignation into the arms of the most holy will of God. It is foolish to imagine that you do not make acts of virtue well; for, as I told you before, they do not cease to be exceedingly good, though performed languidly, heavily, and as if by force. You cannot give God anything but what you have, and, at this season of affliction, you have no other kind of acts.

I suspect that the melancholy humor takes occasion

---

who dispenses you from your practices of piety, or rather who forbids them to you. Hence, be not uneasy, but remember He expects from you in exchange that you will exercise yourself more assiduously in doing His will by renouncing your own, and that it is in order that you may make this exercise your principal nourishment, that the means of doing so are frequently provided for you. Indeed, what contradictions, what reverses, what sacrifices does not sickness entail! Projects disarranged, expenses to be incurred, remedies against which you revolt, awkwardness and negligence on the part of those who have care of you, in fine, a multitude of little things that annoy you! How many occasions of saying: God wishes it to be so. . . . What ought to be your study, then, not to allow a single occasion of this kind to escape, and thus you will deserve to be placed in the rank of those whom Jesus holds most dear; *for whosoever*, He says, *does the will of God, he is my brother, my sister, my mother."*—*Divine Providence.*

from your indisposition to sadden you a good deal, and, seeing yourself sad, you are disquieted; but do not be uneasy,
I beg of you. If you find yourself sluggish, fretful, gloomy,
yet do not fail to remain in peace, and though it seems to
you that everything you do is done without relish, without
sentiment, without energy, still cease not to embrace your
crucified Lord, and to give Him your heart, and to consecrate to Him your spirit with its affections, such as they
are, and languishing though they be. The Blessed Angela of
Foligno said that Our Lord had revealed to her that there is
no kind of good so agreeable to Him as that which is done
perforce, meaning that which a will firmly resolved accom-
plishes in spite of the weariness of the flesh, against the
repugnances of the inferior part of the soul, and in opposition to aridity, sadness, and interior desolation. My God!
My dear daughter, how happy you shall be if you continue
faithful to your resolutions, in the midst of crosses, to Him
who has loved you so faithfully unto death, and even the
death of the cross!

It is a manifest truth that our souls generally contract
in the inferior part the qualities and dispositions of our bodies; and I say in the inferior part, because it is that which is
immediately connected with the body, and subject to share
in the disorders of the body. A delicate body overpowered
by the burden of sickness, grieved by many sorrows, cannot
permit the heart to be so lively, so active, so prompt in its
operations, as in health; but all this does not at all interfere
with the acts of the soul in the superior part, which are as
agreeable to God as if they were made in the midst of the
most joyous gaieties of the world, yea, and more agreeable,

being made with more pain and difficulty; but they are not so agreeable to the person who makes them, because, not entering into the inferior part of the soul, they are not so delectable according to our ideas.

We must not be unjust, nor require from ourselves that which is not in us. When we are inconvenienced in regard to health, we must only require from our spirit some acts of submission, acts of holy union with the good pleasure of God, which are formed in the summit of the soul; and as to exterior actions, we must do the best we can, and content ourselves with performing them, though reluctantly, languidly, and heavily. And to improve the languor, heaviness, and dullness of our heart, making them serviceable to divine love, we must embrace a holy abjection; thus will you change the plummet of your heaviness into gold, and a gold finer than that of the rarest pleasures of the worldly heart. Have patience then with yourself; that the superior part may balance the ponderousness of the inferior part.

Your *Beloved* is a *bouquet of myrrh;* cease not to press this bouquet to your bosom: *my Beloved to me, and I to Him;* He will always be in my heart. Isaias calls Him *the Man of Sorrows.* Torment not yourself to do much, but dispose yourself to suffer with love that which you suffer. God will be propitious to you. Whether languishing, *or living, or dying, we are the Lord's, and nothing shall separate us from His holy love,* through the help of His grace. Never will our heart have life but in Him and for Him. He shall be forever the God of our heart.

Chapter Four

The Book of the Afflicted

I T IS the truth, that nothing in this world can help us to a more profound tranquility than often to look upon Our Lord in the midst of the afflictions which befell Him from His birth until His death; for we shall see there so much poverty, contempt, abjection, calumny, pain, and torment, that we shall be ashamed to call afflictions those little contradictions which we meet with, or to require patience for such trifles, when one single drop of modesty would suffice to make us endure them all well.

A heart that greatly esteems and loves Jesus Christ crucified, loves His death, His pains, His torments, His blows, His opprobriums, His hunger, His thirst, His ignominies; and when it happens to meet with some little participation in them, it thrills with joy, and lovingly embraces them.

I will not tell you not to pay any regard to your afflictions, for your tongue, which is usually prompt at a reply, would inform me that they make themselves to be regarded by the bitterness of the anguish which they produce; but I will rather tell you not to regard them unless in contrast with the cross, for then you will find them either little, or so agreeable that you will prefer to suffer them than to enjoy any consolation separated from them.

The mountain of Calvary is the school of love. There faithful souls discover in the wounds of the Lion of the Tribe of Juda the honey of love; and in Heaven, after the motive of the divine goodness, considered in itself, that of the death of the Saviour will be the most powerful to ravish all the blessed with love. The sacred Passion of Our Lord should be the wellspring and fountain of all our love. The other day, as I was in prayer, considering the open side of Our Lord, and seeing His heart, I fancied that our hearts were there too, all around His, doing it homage as the sovereign King of hearts.

The crucifix is the true book of the Christian. I appeal to you all, O illustrious Doctors of the Church! Whence, O devout St. Bernard, did you draw your sweet doctrine, unless from this book? And you, O pious Augustine, *who didst nourish your soul in the wounds of the Saviour?* And you, O seraphic Francis of Assisi, who extracted from *the book of the cross* so many touching instructions? And you, angelic St. Thomas, who wrote nothing until you had first taken counsel with Jesus crucified? And you, seraphic doctor, St. Bonaventure, who seem in writing your pious little books to have had no other paper than the cross, no other pen than the lance, no other ink than the blood of our Saviour Jesus Christ? Oh, what a fire consumed you, when your heart sent forth this cry of love: "How good it is to be with Jesus crucified! I will make three tabernacles here: one in His hands, another in His feet, and a third in the wounds of His side, where I may watch and repose, read and speak, pray and do everything."[1]

Oh, if Our Lord loved us even to the death of the cross, what remains for us to do but to die of love for Him, or, if we cannot die for Him, at least live only to serve Him? Certainly, if we do not love Him, if we do not live for Him, we are ungrateful and perfidious. "O Lord," said St. Augustine, "is it possible that man can know that Thou hast died for him, and that he will not live for Thee?" "What! My God," said the bleeding St. Francis of Assisi, "Thou hast died of love for us, and no one loves Thee!"

St. Paul, the incomparable master, the great doctor of the infant Church, made Jesus Christ on the cross the delightful object of his love, the sweet subject of his discourses, the end of all his aspirations in this world, and the foundation of all his hopes in eternity. "I have judged myself," he says, "to know nothing but my Jesus crucified; God forbid that I should ever glory in any other thing than in the cross of my Jesus; and think not that I have any other life than that of the cross; for I assure you that I so feel

---

1　St. Bernard studied this great book, I mean the cross of Jesus, with incredible pleasure; he refreshed himself with his Saviour's blood, and with this divine liquor drank in a supreme contempt for the world. "I come," he says, "O good Master, I come to be crucified with Thee. I see that those sweet eyes whose glance cast St. Peter into tears, no longer yield any light; I will close mine forever to the vanity of the world. This divine mouth, from which flowed rivers of living water springing up to eternal life, is shut by death; I will condemn mine to silence, opening it only to confess my sins to Thy mercy. My heart shall be as ice to foolish pleasures, and as I cannot see a single portion of Thy body sound, I wish to carry on every side of me the marks of Thy sufferings, that I may one day be clothed with Thy glorious resurrection."

and behold everywhere the cross of my Saviour, that by His grace I am altogether crucified to the world, and the world is entirely crucified to me." Blessed is the soul which thus everywhere finds Jesus Christ crucified!

It will be useful always to carry the crucifix about with us, to kiss it often with love, to look upon it with respect and tenderness, saying at times:

O Jesus, the beloved of my heart, permit me to press Thee to my breast as a bundle of myrrh; I promise that my mouth, which is so happy as to kiss Thy holy cross, shall abstain from deceits, from murmurs, from every word that might displease Thee; that my eyes, which behold Thy tears and blood flowing for my sins, shall look no more upon the vanities of the world, or anything that might expose me to offend Thee; that my ears, which hear with so much consolation the seven words pronounced on the cross, shall take no more pleasure in empty praise, in useless conversation, in words that wound the neighbor; that my mind, after having studied with so much relish the mystery of the cross, shall be closed against all vain or evil thoughts and imaginations; that my will, submissive to the laws of the cross and to the love of Jesus crucified, shall have only charity towards my brethren; that, in fine, nothing shall enter into or depart from my heart, without the permission of this holy cross, the sacred sign of which I trace upon myself at rising and at going to rest, and in all the sorrows of life."[2]

You ought then every day, not only in prayer, but even while walking, take a view of Our Lord enduring the pains

---

2   "Behold my book!" said the angelic Pius VII, showing his crucifix, when Napoleon asked him what he read during the long hours of his sorrowful captivity.

of our redemption, and consider what a happiness it will be for you to participate in them. Examine on what occasions the like may happen to you, such as contradictions to your desires, even those desires which appear to you most just and legitimate; and then, with a great love for the cross and Passion of Our Lord, cry out with St. Andrew: "O good cross! So much loved by my Saviour, when will you receive me into your arms?"

What a grace, to be not only under the cross, but on the cross, and at least a little crucified with Our Lord! Have good courage, make a virtue of necessity, and lose not an opportunity of showing your love for God in the midst of tribulation, as He in the midst of thorns has shown His for you.

Remain in peace in the paternal arms of the most loving care which God has of you, and will have of you, since you belong to Him, and are no longer your own. Oh, how great a favor it is, when He reserves His consolations for the life to come!

The present life is such that in it we must use the bread of bitterness more than honey; but that life for which we have resolved to cherish holy patience will abundantly repay us in due season. "Beware," says the Apostle, "of losing confidence, by which being fortified, you shall valiantly support the combat of afflictions, however great they may be." [3]

---

3 The cross is engraven everywhere; the things of this world carry its impress, and God has arranged matters so that we may be always prepared to receive it.

   We must not reject the cross when it appears, and it will always appear; we shall always suffer. Does not our own experience prove the immense need we have of suffering? If by an impossibility, a soul were exempt from suffering, where would be its

When the wind blows in our valleys, between the lofty mountains, it bends the little flowers and tears up the great trees. So I, who dwell a little high up in the office of bishop, am exposed to more inconveniences. . . . But at the foot of the sacred cross of Our Lord, the rain which falls on all sides abates the wind. When I am there, O God, how much my heart is at peace, and what sweetness proceeds from that vermilion dew! Let us then remain always in the pierced side of our Saviour. . . . How good is the Lord! How amiable is His heart! Let us remain in this holy asylum, let this Heart ever live in our hearts, and let this blood ever bound through the veins of our souls.

Place your head at the foot of the cross, and keep it there humbly and full of confidence, to receive the merits of the Precious Blood which will flow down upon it.

---

virtue? Where would be its sanctity? We shall be able to suffer when we understand that suffering is the work of God, and the means chosen by God to lead us to Him.

CHAPTER FIVE

THE SICK WHO CANNOT PRAY

ALL *things have their time.* There is a time to suffer, and a time to pray. It is not during spring or winter we seek for fruit on trees. We should have flesh of iron, to act in suffering or to suffer in acting. When God calls us to suffer, He does not require us to act.

There are some sick persons who, seeing themselves stretched on a bed of pain, complain, not so much indeed of their sorrows as of their inability to render Our Lord the services they were accustomed to render Him in health. In acting thus, they greatly deceive themselves, for one hour of suffering through love and submission to the will of God, is worth more than many days of labor with less love.

But now for the truth: we always wish to serve God in our own way, not in His; according to our own will, not according to His; and we love His will when it is conformable to ours, instead of loving ours only when and inasmuch as it is conformable to His.

35

When He wishes us to be sick, we wish to be well. When He desires us to serve Him by suffering, we desire to serve Him by action. When He wishes us to practice patience, we wish to practice humility, devotion, prayer, or some other virtue, not because it is more to His liking, but more to ours. We love virtue when accompanied with sweet sauce, not when accompanied with vinegar and gall. Calvary does not agree so well with us as Thabor; it is not on the former mountain, but on the latter, we would wish to build our tabernacles.

In a word, we prefer health to sickness, and we do not love God the same in health and in sickness. We love Him better when He caresses us than when He strikes us, and thus we change, and, instead of loving the love of God, we love the sweetness of His love; for he who loves only God, loves Him equally at all times, in sickness and in health, in prosperity and in adversity, in suffering and in joy. God being always the same, the variation of our love towards Him cannot but proceed from something out of Him.

Chapter Six

Advice to Convalescents

WHILE our bodies are in pain, it is difficult to elevate our hearts to the perfect consideration of the goodness of Our Lord; so great a perfection belongs only to those who, from long habit, have their minds entirely turned towards Heaven. But we, who are yet too tender, have souls that are easily turned aside by the thought of labors and bodily fatigues. On which account, it is no wonder if, during your sickness, you omit the exercise of mental prayer, as, at that time, it is sufficient to employ ejaculatory prayers and pious aspirations; and, since the sickness makes us often sigh, it costs us nothing more to sigh in God, to God, and for God, than to sigh in useless complaints.

But now that God has restored your health, it is necessary, my dear daughter, to resume your prayer, at least for half an hour in the morning and a quarter of an hour in the evening before supper; for, since Our Lord has once given you a relish for this heavenly honey, it would be a great reproach in you to disrelish it, and especially since He made you enjoy it with so much facility and consolation, as I very well remember you told me He did. We must then have courage, and not allow anything to deprive us of so rich a treat as is that of conversing heart to heart with God.

CHAPTER SEVEN

NEITHER TO DESIRE NOR TO REFUSE COMFORT IN SICKNESS

OUR Lord, when on the cross, showed us how to mortify those sentiments of nature which make us too tender about ourselves; for, being very thirsty, He did not ask a drink, but only manifested His want, saying, "I thirst." After that He made an act of the greatest submission; for one of those present offering Him a sponge steeped in vinegar on the end of a lance, He tasted it with His blessed lips.

A strange thing! He was not ignorant that such a beverage would increase His anguish; nevertheless, He took it without a word, to teach us with what submission we should receive what is presented to us in sickness, without manifesting our repugnance or our disgust.

Alas! If we are much or little inconvenienced, far from imitating our sweet Master, we never cease to lament and complain; our sickness, whatever it is, is extraordinary, and that which others suffer is nothing in comparison with it; we are more vexed and impatient than can be described; and we can find nothing to relieve us soon enough. Truly it is a great pity to see how little we imitate the patience of our Saviour, who, forgetting His sorrows, did not endeavor to have them observed, but was content, that His heavenly Father, by whose order He suffered them, considered them, and would pour out their fruit on mankind, for whom they were endured.

It is true, indeed, that humility, patience, and the love of Him who sends us crosses, require that we should receive them without complaint; but see, my dearest daughter, there is a difference between telling one's affliction and complaining of it. We can tell it: on many occasions we are obliged to tell it, as we are obliged to remedy it; but this ought to be done peacefully, without increasing it by exaggerations or lamentations.

This is what St. Teresa says; for it is not to complain, to tell one's sickness; but to tell it with sighs, with groans, with many evidences of sorrow, is reprehensible. Tell it then simply and truthfully, without scruple; in such a manner, that you may not seem unwilling to be sweetly resigned to it, as you ought to be.

Engrave then on your memory these two precious maxims, which I have already so often recommended to you: Desire nothing, refuse nothing. Look upon the little Jesus in the crib; He receives poverty, nakedness, the society of beasts, the inclemency of the weather, and all that His Father permits to happen to Him. It is not written that He ever reached out His hands to be lifted up into the bosom of His Mother. He abandoned Himself entirely to her care and her foresight. He did not refuse the little comforts she gave Him, and received the services of St. Joseph, the adoration and presents of the shepherds and the kings, all with a holy equanimity. We ought to act in like manner, and, after the example of our divine Saviour, neither ask anything nor refuse anything, but be equally willing to suffer and to receive whatever the Providence of God may permit to befall us. May God grant us the grace to do so!

of His Mother. He abandoned Himself entirely to her care and her friendship. He did not refuse the little comforts she gave Him, and received the services of St. Joseph, the aid rendered means of the shepherds and the Christians, all with a holy equanimity. We ought to act in like manner, and imitate the example of our divine Saviour, neither asking thing, nor refuse anything; but be equally willing, to suffer and to receive whatever the Providence of God may permit us to befall us. May God grant us the grace to do so!

CHAPTER EIGHT

PATIENCE IN SICKNESS

I FIND in the Gospel a perfect model of this virtue in the person of St. Peter's mother-in-law. This good woman, attacked by a heavy fever, remained tranquil and peaceful, without any uneasiness herself, and without causing any to those around her. She was content to suffer her malady in patience and in meekness. O God! How happy she was, and how well she deserved to be taken care of, for the Apostles obtained her cure without being solicited by her, impelled only by a motive of charity and compassion to relieve her.

This dear patient knew well that Our Lord was at Capharnaum, and that He cured the sick; nevertheless, she was not anxious to send a messenger to tell Him of what she suffered. But what is still more admirable is, that she saw Him in her house, where He looked upon her, and she also looked upon Him; and yet she did not say a single word to excite Him to compassion, nor did she put herself in the way of touching Him in order to be cured.

Still more, she did not appear to make any account of her malady, she was not affected in describing it, she did not complain of it, she did not ask anyone to pity her or to obtain her cure. She was content that God, and those who governed her, knew it. She regarded Our Lord not only as her sovereign physician, but also as her God, to whom she belonged equally in health and in sickness, being as content in sickness as in health.

Oh, how many persons would have had the cleverness to try to get cured by Our Lord, and would have said that they asked health only the better to serve Him, fearing lest anything should be wanting to Him! But this holy woman did not think of that, showing her resignation, and asking nothing of Our Lord, but His most holy will.

Yet I do not mean to say that we cannot make a petition to Our Lord, with this condition: "If such be His will." It is not sufficient to be sick because God wishes it, but we must also be content to suffer it as He wishes, when He wishes, during the time He wishes, and in the manner He wishes, making no choice or refusal of any malady, however abject or humiliating it may be; for sickness without abjection often inflates the heart instead of humbling it. But when accompanied with confusion, what an opportunity of practicing patience, humility, and meekness of spirit and of heart!

Let us then have a great care, after the example of this holy woman, to keep our heart in meekness, turning our maladies to advantage as she did; for, being cured, she arose immediately and served Our Lord, using her health only for His good pleasure. In this generous forgetfulness of self, she did not imitate those persons of the world, who, having been sick for a few days, take weeks and months to recover.

As to the afflictions of your heart, you can easily discern those for which there is a remedy, from those for which there is none. Where there is a remedy, you should endeavor peacefully and sweetly to procure it; and where there is not, you should endure the affliction as a mortification which Our Lord sends upon you, in order to exercise you, and make you entirely His own.

Beware of yielding to complaints; rather oblige your heart to suffer tranquilly; and if it happens to make some sally of impatience, restore it to peace and meekness. Believe me, God loves the souls that are agitated by the waves and tempests of this world, provided they receive their tribulations from His hands, and, like valiant warriors, endeavor to maintain their fidelity amid a thousand dangers.

I should not wonder if, henceforward, age and the nature of your constitution, would often cause you to be delicate; and, therefore, I advise you to exercise yourself much in the love of the most amiable will of God, in the renunciation of exterior comforts, and in sweetness in the midst of bitterness; you cannot make a more excellent sacrifice. Hold fast to it, and practice not only a solid love, but a tender, sweet, and gentle love towards those around you: I say this from the experience I have had, that infirmities, though never depriving us of charity, take away, nevertheless, a spirit of gentleness towards the neighbor, unless we are greatly on our guard against them.

Chapter Nine

Patience in Painful Operations

MAY Our Lord be pleased to give us His Holy Spirit, to do and suffer all things according to His holy will! I come to your sore leg, and find that it must be opened; this cannot be done without extreme pain. But, my God! What an occasion of trial has His goodness give us in this necessity! Oh! Courage, we belong to Jesus Christ; behold how He clothes us with His livery. Imagine that the instrument to open your leg is one of those nails that pierced the feet of Our Lord.

Oh, what a happiness! He chose favors of this kind for Himself, and so much cherished them that He has borne marks of them into Paradise, and now He sends you a share of them. But you will tell me that you cannot serve God while you lie in bed; and I reply: "When did Our Lord render the greatest service to His Father?" Undoubtedly when He was laid upon the bed of the cross, having His hands and feet pierced. This was the greatest act of His service.

Behold, your cross has come to you; embrace and caress it for the love of Him who sends it to you. The afflicted David said to God: "I am dumb, and I open not my mouth, because Thou hast done it;" as if he should say: "If anyone else, O my God, had sent me this affliction, I would not like it, I would resent it; but since Thou hast sent it, I say not a word, I accept it, I receive it, I honor it."[1]

We are in this world only to receive and to carry the sweet Jesus: on our tongue, by announcing Him; on our arms, by doing good works; on our shoulders, by bearing His yoke, His aridities, and His trials; and as well in our interior senses are we to carry Him, as in our exterior ones. Oh, how blessed are they who carry Him lovingly and constantly!

But here is a precious balm to sweeten your sorrows. Every day take a drop or two of the blood which distils from the wounds in the feet of Our Lord, and receive it into your soul by meditation; with your imagination, also, dip your finger reverently in this liquor, and apply it to your affliction, invoking the sweet name of Jesus: and you will find that your grief will diminish.

The obedience which you render the doctor will be exceedingly agreeable to God, and will be put to your credit on the Day of Judgment.

---

1 The glorious martyr, St. Gordius, said to his executioners, in order to excite and stimulate their sloth: "Tear my body, cut it into little morsels, make me suffer everything you wish, grudge me not the hope of beatitude: the more you crush my body under blows, the more you increase my recompense." The sorrows we endure for the love of God are like contracts that we make with Him. For wounds and bruises, He obliges Himself to clothe us with a shining robe; for affronts, He will give us a crown of glory; for a prison, the vast empire of Heaven; for the wicked sentence passed against our innocence, we shall hear the praises and benedictions of angels and saints.

Whilst confined to your bed, I bear you a particular respect, and a more than ordinary esteem, as a person visited by God, clothed in His habit, and His special spouse.

When Our Lord was on the cross, He was declared king, even by His enemies; and souls that are on the cross are declared queens.

St. Paul, who had been in Heaven, and in the midst of the felicities of Paradise, regarded himself as happy only in his infirmities, and on the cross of Our Lord.

When your leg is lanced, say with the same Apostle: "Let no one any more annoy or trouble me; for I carry the marks and signs of my Saviour in my body."

O fortunate limb, which, being well turned to account, will carry you farther into Heaven, than if it were the soundest in the world!

Paradise is a mountain towards which we walk better with bruised and broken legs, than with leg sound and entire.

Chapter Ten

Perseverance in Patience

"IN YOUR patience," says the Son of God, "you shall possess your souls." It is then the effect of patience to possess one's soul well, and in proportion as patience is greater, the possession of the soul will be fuller and more excellent; besides, patience is so much the more perfect as it is the less blended with fretfulness and anxiety. From these two last inconveniences may God be pleased to deliver you, and very soon after you will be quite at peace.

Good courage, I beg of you. You have only suffered the hardship of the way for three years, and you would wish for repose; but remember two things: one, the children of Israel were forty years in the desert before arriving in the land of rest, which had been promised to them, though six weeks would have sufficed for the journey at their ease, and it was not lawful for them to inquire why God obliged them to make so many windings, and to pass through such rough trials, while all those who murmured died on the way; the other, Moses, the greatest friend of God in the whole multitude, died on the frontiers of the promised land, seeing it with his eyes, and being unable to enjoy it.

May God help us to regard little the nature of the way that we tread, but to keep our eyes fixed on Him who leads us, and on the blessed country to which He leads us! What matter, whether we pass through deserts or through fields, provided God is with us, and we go to Heaven. I beg of you to elude the remembrance of your malady as much as you can, and though you feel it, you need not consider or look upon it; for the sight of it will give you more apprehension than the thought of it would give you grief. Thus we bandage the eyes of those on whom the sword or the lance has to be used. It seems to me that you dwell a little too long on the consideration of your ailment.

And as for what you tell me, that it is very distressing to you to wish to act, and to be unable to act, I do not mean to say that we should wish to do that which we cannot do; but I mean to tell you that it is a great power before God to have the power to wish. Pass on further, I beseech you, and think on the great dereliction which our Master suffered in the Garden of Olives, and see how this dear Son having asked consolation of His good Father, who was unwilling to bestow it, He thought no more of it, sought it no more, was no more uneasy; but, as if He had never desired it, accomplished valiantly and courageously the work of our redemption.

After you have prayed the Father to console you, if He is not pleased to do so, think no more of it; but rouse your courage to complete the work of your salvation on the cross, as if you were never to descend from it, and as if the atmosphere of your life were nevermore to be clear and serene. What would you wish? We must know how to speak to God in the thunder and in the whirlwind; we must look upon Him in the bush in the midst of fire and thorns; and to do this, we must take the shoes off our feet, and practice a great abnegation of our will and affections. But the goodness of God has not called you into His company, without strengthening you for all this. It is for Him to perfect His task. Truly it is a little long, for so the matter requires; but—patience!

In short, for the honor of God, acquiesce entirely in His will, and do not for a moment suppose that you can serve Him better otherwise; for we never serve Him well, unless we serve Him as He wishes.

Now He wishes you to serve Him without relish, without enjoyment, with repugnances and convulsions of the soul. This service gives you no satisfaction, but it contents Him; it is not to your liking, but it is to His.

Granting that you were never to be delivered from your anguishes, what ought you to do? You ought to say to God: "I am Thine; if my miseries are pleasing to Thee, increase them in number and in duration." I have confidence in Our Lord that you will say this, and think no more of them; at least that you will not be uneasy. Act in this manner now, and tame yourself to pains, as if you were always to live in them; you will find that when you think no more of your deliverance, God will think of it, and when you make no hurry about it, He will run to you.

CHAPTER ELEVEN

EXCESSIVE FEAR OF DEATH[1]

IN OUR language, we call those who are dead the departed, as if we meant to say that they had passed from this life to a better; and, to speak the truth, the sojourn we make on earth during the days of our mortality, and to which we give the name of life, is rather a death than life, since every moment of it leads us to the tomb.

---

1 "Let us have great ideas and noble sentiments on the goodness of God; let us be filled with confidence in Him, and He will manifest Himself to us, and the sight of Him, which in this world is only an impress of His presence, elevating our souls to Him, will replenish us with joy. We ought especially to inspire the sick with this confidence and joy, their dejection rendering them more susceptible of impressions of fear, which is the beginning of sadness. Weakness of body conducts to timidity of soul, as we see in children and in old people. Above all, we should inspire the dying with this confidence, and they cannot be too much inspired with it, particularly if they belong to that class who have great reason to fear the judgments of God. The devil drives them along towards the abyss of despair, and the decline is rapid. We must fear during life, and hope much at death. When we are full of health and strength, it is necessary that fear should restrain our inconstancy and humble our pride. In the dying man, we have to fear neither presumption nor relapse. His sins will end with his life, and the dread of the judgments of God gives no room to look for presumption."—*P. Lambez.*

This made an ancient philosopher say that we die every day, for every day takes away a portion of our life. Hence that beautiful expression of the wise Thecuan woman: "We all die, and we are on the earth like rivers that flow on to be engulfed in the sea."

Nature has impressed on all men a horror of death; the Saviour Himself, espousing our flesh and becoming like to His brethren, sin excepted, would not exempt Himself from this infirmity, although He knew that this passage would set Him free from human miseries, and transfer Him to a glory which He possessed already, as far as His soul was concerned.

One of the ancients said that death ought not to be esteemed an evil, or regarded as unpleasant, when it has been preceded by a good life; for nothing makes it terrible unless that which follows it.

Against the fears that spring from the apprehension of the divine judgments, we have the buckler of a blessed hope, which makes us cast all our confidence, not on our own virtue, but on the mercy of God alone, assuring us that those who trust in His goodness shall never be confounded in their expectations.

I have committed many faults, it is true; but where is the foolish person who would think it in his power to commit more than God could forgive? And who will dare to measure, by the greatness of his crimes, the immensity of that infinite mercy which casts them all into the depths of the sea of oblivion, when we repent of them with love? It belongs only to madmen, like Cain, to say that their sin is too great to be forgiven; *because with the Lord there is mercy, and with Him plentiful redemption: He shall redeem Israel from all his iniquities.*

It is true, indeed, that at the sight of our past sins, we ought always to be in fear and in sorrow; but we should not remain thus, we should pass beyond this resting place, and call faith, hope, and charity to our assistance; then our most bitter sorrow will be changed into peace, our servile fear will become chaste and filial, and distrust of ourselves, like a piece of exceeding bitter aloes, will be sweetened by the sugar of confidence in God.

He who tarries at diffidence and fear alone, without passing on to hope and confidence, resembles him who, from a rose tree, would cull only the thorns, and leave the roses. We must imitate surgeons, who never open the veins unless the bandages for stopping the blood are all ready. *He who confides in God shall be as Mount Sion, which is never moved by the storm.*

Chapter Twelve

Remedies against Excessive Fear of Death

WHOEVER has a true desire of serving Our Lord, and avoiding sin, ought on no account to be afflicted by the thought of death or of the divine judgments; for, though both are to be feared, yet fear ought not to be of that terrifying nature which destroys the energy of the soul, but ought to be so blended with confidence in the goodness of God, that by this means it may become sweet.

Behold some efficacious remedies for diminishing an excessive fear of death:

The first is perseverance in the service of God. I assure you that if you persevere in the exercise of devotion, as I perceive you do, you will find yourself greatly relieved from this torment; for your soul, keeping itself exempt from evil affections, and uniting itself more and more to God, will find itself less attached to this mortal life, and to all vain complacency in it.

Continue then in a devout life, as you have begun, and advance always from good to better, in the way in which you walk; and you will see that, after a time, those alarms will grow less, and you will not be disquieted so much.

Consider sometimes that you are a child of the Catholic Church, and rejoice in the thought; for the children of this mother who desire to live according to her laws, always die happy, and, as the blessed mother Teresa says, it is a great consolation at the hour of death to be a child of Holy Church.[1]

Finish all your prayers with acts of confidence, saying: "Lord, Thou art my hope; on Thee I have cast my confidence. Whoever hoped in God, and was disappointed? I hope in Thee, O Lord, and I shall never be confounded." In ejaculatory prayers during the day, and in the reception of the Most Blessed Sacrament, always use words of love and hope towards Our Lord, such as: "Thou art my Father, O Lord; O God, the spouse of my love, Thou art the king of my heart, and the beloved of my soul; O sweet Jesus, Thou art my dear master, my support, my refuge."

Better not read books, or portions of books, in which death, judgment, and Hell are treated of; because, thanks be to God, you have fully resolved to live in a Christian

---

1 "How sweet it will be for us at the hour of death to see that we go to be judged by Him whom we have loved above all things! With what confidence may we present ourselves before Him, sure of receiving a favorable sentence from His mouth! What ineffable happiness to think that we do not go to a strange land, but to our true country, since it is that of the celestial spouse whom we so much love, and by whom we are so much loved."—*St. Teresa of Avila.*

manner, and have no need of being impelled to it by motives of fear and terror.

The second remedy is the frequent remembrance of the great sweetness and mercy with which God, our Saviour, receives souls on their departure, when they have confided themselves to Him during life, and endeavored to serve and love Him, everyone according to his vocation.

The third is love of Paradise; for, in proportion as we esteem and love eternal felicity, we shall have less regret in quitting this mortal life.

The fourth is a certain intimacy with the blessed, often invoking and addressing them with words of praise and affection; for, having thus a familiar intercourse with the citizens of the celestial Jerusalem, it will grieve us less to part with those of the terrestrial. These, and the like considerations, carefully meditated on for some time, will greatly diminish an excessive dread of the divine judgments, and lead us to hope confidently that, being children of a Father so rich in goodness as to love us, and to wish to save us, so enlightened as to know the means suitable to this end, so wise as to arrange them, so powerful as to see them carried into effect, He will not wish to condemn us, so long as we do that which we are able in His divine service.[2]

Often adore, praise, and bless the most holy death of our crucified Lord, and place all your confidence in His

---

2   "O my daughters, let us not desire to live at our ease, while we are here: one night in a bad wayside inn is all. Let us praise God, and endeavor to do penance in this life. Oh, how sweet will be the death of the sister, who, having done penance in this world for all her sins, will not have to pass through Purgatory! Yes, it may happen that from this land of exile, she will enter straight into the enjoyment of glory. Nothing will trouble her; she will taste a celestial peace."—*St. Teresa of Avila.*

merits, by which your death will be made happy; and often
say: "O divine death of my sweet Jesus, bless mine, and it
will be blessed; I bless Thee, and Thou wilt bless me. O
death more amiable than life!" Thus St. Charles, during the
sickness of which he died, caused a picture of Our Lord's
burial, and another of His agony in the Garden of Olives,
to be placed before him, that he might console himself with
the remembrance of the Passion and death of his Redeemer.

Certainly, since Jesus Christ has died, we ought never
to wish ill to death, or represent to ourselves the judgment
on one side, without the cross of our Saviour on the other,
in order that, after having been excited to a holy fear by the
remembrance of our sins, we may be restored to peace by
confidence in our Redeemer.[3]

Lift up your heart often towards Jesus by a holy confidence, blended with a holy humility, saying:

> I am miserable, O Lord, but Thou wilt
> receive my misery into the bosom of Thy
> mercy, and Thou wilt bring me, with Thy
> paternal hand, to the joy of Thy inheri-
> tance. I am contemptible, vile, and abject;
> but Thou wilt love me this day, because I

---

3   What can be more touching than the words of Bossuet, describing, before the most
celebrated court in the world, the last moments of Henrietta of England?

"It seem as if God had preserved her judgment clear until the last breath, that she
might continue to give testimonies of her faith. Dying, she loved the Saviour Jesus.
Her arms rather than her desires failed her, to embrace the crucifix. I have seen her
trembling hand struggle, as it fell, for new strength to apply to her lips the blessed
sign of our redemption. Is not this to die amid the embraces and the kisses of the
Lord? Ah! We can complete with a pious confidence this holy sacrifice for her repose.
Jesus, in whom she hoped, whose cross she carried in her body by so many cruel
pains, will give her again His Blood, with which she has been already so deeply tinc-
tured, by participation in His Sacraments and by communication in His sufferings."

have hoped in Thee, and have desired to be
Thine.

It is true, death is hideous; but that life which is beyond the grave, and which the mercy of God will give us, is very desirable. We must by no means fall into diffidence; for, though we are sinners, yet we are far from being as bad as God is merciful to forgive those who repent, who have a will to amend, and who place their hopes in Jesus Christ. Death is no longer ignominious, but glorious, since the Son of God has undergone it. Hence the Blessed Virgin, and all the saints, have esteemed it an advantage to die, after the example of the Saviour, who allowed Himself, of His own free consent, to be attached to the cross; and death has become through Jesus Christ so sweet and amiable, that the angels would regard themselves happy if they could have the privilege of enduring it.[4]

We must die! These words are hard, but they are followed by a great happiness: it is in order to be with God that we die. You ought to be aware that no sensible person puts new wine into old vessels; the liquor of divine love cannot enter where the old Adam reigns.

Often consider the persons whom you most love, and from whom it would most grieve you to be separated, as those with whom you will be eternally united in Heaven:

---

4 "It is vain for those of a sincere faith to say that they do not wish to die so soon, in order that they may have time to become better; for they will not advance in virtue unless in proportion as they advance in the disposition which makes one desire death. To desire not to die is not a means to acquire more virtue; it is rather a mark that we have scarcely acquired any. Let those therefore who do not desire to die, in order that they may be able to become perfect, desire to die, and they will then be perfect."—*St. Augustine.*

for example, your husband, your little John, your father. "Oh, this little boy, through the help of God, will one day be happy in eternal life, in which he will enjoy my felicity and rejoice in it, and I shall enjoy his and rejoice in it, without our ever more being separated!" The same with regard to your husband, your father, and others.

Let us walk, then, with confidence, under the standard of God's Providence, without yielding to those fears which might trouble us; for, if we think on death with uneasiness, the thought will be more injurious than advantageous to us. Let us think on it with peace and tranquility of mind, reposing on the bosom of Providence, without putting ourselves in pain to know when we shall die or where, whether by an accident or not, suddenly or after a long illness, attended by others or not, confiding all to the goodness of God. Do we not see that He has care of the birds of heaven, and not one of their feathers falls to the ground without His leave? He knows the number of hairs on your head, and not one of them falls without His will. I wish, we ought to say, to belong entirely to God, not only from a sense of duty, but much more from affection. And, provided I accomplish His most holy will, what else have I to do but to abandon myself to His good Providence, full of confidence that He will have care of me in life and at death?

St. Augustine says that to die well it is necessary to live well, and such as our life is, such will be our death. These words are common and apparently trivial, but they contain a great lesson. Live well, and you will not fear death, or if you fear it, it will be with a sweet and tranquil fear;

relying on the merits of the Passion of Our Lord, without which, indeed, death would be frightful and terrible to all men.

God will aid us provided we pray to Him,[5] since He has left us so many means of dying well, particularly that of contrition, which is so general and so efficacious as to efface all kinds of sins, and also the Sacraments, by which we are restored to grace and washed from the guilt of sin; for the Sacraments are like channels by which the merits of the Passion of Our Lord flow into our souls.[6]

Since then Our Lord has given us so many means of being saved, and since He desires our salvation more than we can desire it ourselves, what remains for us to do, unless to abandon ourselves to the guidance of His Divine Providence, seeking nothing, and refusing nothing? Oh, how

---

5 "You will desire at the hour of death that confidence you have previously experienced: are you ignorant that what we have during the course of life will have its effect at death? What are we doing but dying? Cannot He who gives us confidence continue it? What will the soul do at the last hour, unless that which it has always been doing? Are not all moments in the power of God, and is there one of them which may not be the moment of death? What should be done, then, at every moment, but extend our confidence to the succeeding moments, and even to all eternity, if our life could continue so long?"—*Bossuet.*

6 "It is by the last grace that death changes its nature for Christians, since, while it seems to divest us of everything, it really begins, as the Apostle says (*2 Cor.* 5:3), to clothe us, securing to us the eternal possession of true goods. So long as we are detained in this mortal abode, we live subject to change, because, if you allow me to use the expression, change is the law of the country in which we dwell, and we possess no good, even in the order of grace, which we may not lose a moment after, by the natural mutability of our desires. But as soon as we cease to count the hours, and to measure our life by days and years, issuing from figures which pass and shadows which disappear, we arrive at the kingdom of truth, where we are set free from the law of change. Then our soul is no more in danger, our resolutions no longer vacillate, death, or rather the grace of final perseverance, has power to fix them, and as the testament of Jesus Christ, by which He gave Himself to us, was confirmed forever, according to the nature of testaments and the doctrine of the Apostle (*Heb.* 9:15), by the death of this divine testator, so the death of the faithful causes the blessed testament by which we give ourselves to the Saviour to become irrevocable."—*Bossuet.*

happy are they who live in this holy indifference, and who, awaiting what God will arrange for them, prepare themselves by a good life for a good death!

The bed of a good death ought to have for its mattress the love of God; but it is proper to have the head reclining on two pillows, which are humility and confidence in the divine mercy.[7]

---

7   "The first of these pillows, which is humility, makes us know our misery, and inspires us with a salutary fear; but this humility is at the same time courageous and generous, so that while it casts us down, it also raises us up, by faith in the Almighty, making us rely upon Him alone; thus the first of these pillows conducts us to the second, which is that of confidence in God. Now, what is this confidence, unless a hope strengthened by the consideration of the infinite goodness of our Heavenly Father, who desires our welfare more than we can desire it ourselves? *O my God, I have hoped in Thee, and I shall never be confounded.*"—*De Baudry.*

CHAPTER THIRTEEN

GOD DOES NOT ABANDON
US AT THE HOUR OF DEATH

AS A gentle mother, leading her little child with her, helps it to walk, carries it according as she sees necessity, allows it to make some steps by itself in places which are very smooth, and not at all dangerous, sometimes taking it by the hand and steadying it, sometimes lifting it up in her arms and carrying it for a while; so Our Lord has a continual care over the guidance of His children, that is to say, of those who have charity, making them walk before Him, reaching them His hand in difficulties, and carrying them Himself in trials which He sees would otherwise be insupportable to them. This He has declared by Isaias: "I am thy God, taking thee by the hand, and saying to thee: Fear nothing, for I have helped thee." And this conduct, full of sweetness, God observes in regard to our souls from their introduction into charity until their final perfection, which is effected only at the hour of death. *He who perseveres to the end will be saved.*

Finally, the celestial King, having guided the soul which He loves even to the end of life, assists it still in its blessed departure, by which He draws it to the nuptial bed of eternal glory, which is the delightful reward of holy perseverance. And then the soul, all ravished with love for its Beloved, representing to itself the multitude of favors and helps by which He has prevented and assisted it during the days of its pilgrimage, kisses incessantly the sweet succoring hand that led it along the way, and confesses that it is from our divine Saviour alone it holds all its happiness, since He has done for it all that which the great patriarch Jacob desired for his journey, when he beheld the ladder from Heaven. "O Lord," it then says, "Thou hast been with me, and hast kept me in the way by which I have come; Thou hast given me the bread of Thy Sacraments for my nourishment; Thou hast clothed me with the nuptial robe of charity; Thou hast brought me into this abode of glory which is Thy house, O my Eternal Father! What, O Lord, remains, unless for me to declare that Thou art my God, forever and ever?" *Amen.*

Such is the order of our progress to eternal life, for the accomplishment of which Divine Providence has established from eternity a multitude, a distinction, and a succession of necessary graces, with the dependence which they have one upon another.

CHAPTER FOURTEEN

GOD WILL NEVER DESTROY A
SOUL SUBMISSIVE TO HIS WILL

WE DEAL with a Master who is rich in mercy to those who invoke Him; He forgives a debt of ten thousand talents on a small petition. We must have sentiments worthy of His goodness; we must serve Him with fear; but while we tremble, we must not cease to rejoice. The humility that discourages is not a good humility.

God loves us; He knows what we require better than we do ourselves. Whether we live or die we are the Lord's. To Him belong the keys of life and death; those who hope in Him shall never be confounded.

Let us not amuse ourselves so much with trifles; let us look only to His most holy will. Let this be our beautiful star; it will guide us to Jesus Christ, either in the crib or on Calvary. He who follows it will not walk in darkness, but will have the light of eternal life, which is not subject to death.

Although God is omnipotent and there is nothing impossible to Him, yet in His mercy He has bound Himself not to destroy forever a soul whose will, at its exit from the body, is submissive to His will. As the tree falls, so it lies; and the soul will remain forever in that state in which it is found at the end of life; if rebellious to the will of God, its portion will be the chalice of the wicked, and in the lake of fire and brimstone; if submissive to His holy will, its salvation is unquestionable, though a delay may be made in Purgatory, while some rust is burning away, since nothing defiled can enter Heaven. So that, by unreservedly abandoning oneself into the arms of God during life and at death, there is nothing to fear; because, besides that His will ought to be our satisfaction, and He does not desire that anyone should perish, but that all should come to salvation by penance, *therefore it is that He will never send a soul submissive to His will into exterior darkness, which is prepared only for rebels to His light and to His love.*

Chapter Fifteen

Sentiments at the Sight of Death

AFTER having been tossed about on the sea of the world, and having encountered so many perils from the tempest of vanity, which again and again threatened me with shipwreck, I present myself at last before Thee, O my God, to render Thee an account of the talent with which Thy infinite goodness has entrusted me. I now behold the earth which I have been so sorry to think of leaving behind me, and the risks that poor mortals run. How false are the charms of the world! How powerful are its attractions! How deceitful are its allurements! How sweet its honey appears to the eye, though it has the sourness of vinegar! Prepare thyself, O my soul, to go to the heavenly Jerusalem. Behold the end of life: it has no other work than that of death, and a well-regulated devotion produces no other result than eternal life. This is the autumn in which we gather the fruits of eternity. The plant, which has received its increase from heaven, will soon be plucked; and mortals will no longer behold anything of it on earth save the roots, the sad remnants of corruption. The flower, which the sun has painted with various colors, will soon fade away. Consider that life flies as a shadow, passes as a dream, evaporates as smoke; human ambition cannot lay hold on anything solid. All is transitory.

The sun, which rises on our horizon, hastens his course and pursues the night, and the night solicits the light to come in order to roll even the most beautiful portions of the universe into a kind of nothingness—I mean the starry heavens. The rivers flow on to the ocean as if the ocean, which is their center, ought to give them repose. The moon appears on high, sometimes full, sometimes on her decline, and seems to be pleased, as if she were about to finish her labors and her course. The winter deprives the trees of their honor, in order to give us a lesson on death. I am no longer attached to earth by any tie or affection. I have resigned all my desires into Thy hands, O my God; for a long time Thou hast been teaching me to die. The sentiments of the world, which are now dead in me, have taught me the lesson of death.

Mortifications of the spirit have weakened my body. I have not lived of late, since I have been dead by design and determination; I have esteemed nothing life but that which is in Thee. I could not call myself alive, since all my intentions were to extinguish that fire which constitutes the life of worldlings, in order to form my existence to death, or rather to a sweet sleep, in which I should endeavor to unite myself to Thee, and to approach to eternal life. But, O my God, how vain and illusive have been my plans! I did not consider formerly that it was necessary to die actually in order to approach to Thy grandeur and enjoy the bliss of beatitude. Now at dissolution, the raptures of my soul present me with a sample of what is at hand. I have no more faith in ecstasies, for I see; I have no more hope, for I begin to possess; and charity alone remains to unite me to Thee, Who art charity itself, whence proceeds the fire of love which consumes the hearts of the devout. And as fire, of its own nature, mounts upward, so my heart, burning with charity, flies towards Thee; and the more I perceive the powers of my body to become enfeebled, the more my spirit is fortified. In this state, I can see as in a mirror the nature of beatitude.

How indescribable are the joys and delights of a soul that is in the state of grace! Sensual pleasures bring satiety, an evidence of their imperfection; but the contentments of the soul are infinite, always increase the appetite, and never lose their sweetness, because they have no end, and are not limited by the senses, or by sensible objects.

Let us go forth then from this world, and ascend to Heaven, by the help of the mercy of God. And you, devout souls, are you not content to follow me? Do you fear the passage? Are you not dead in God, to be resuscitated glorious? Am I to believe that you are still alive, since you are without will, without affection, having renounced yourselves to embrace the word, and the commandments which Heaven has dictated to you? You fear the evil of dissolution: consider that Our Lord suffered so great a pain for you.

You fear to quit the medleys of the world, where vanity reigns, where avarice tarnishes the most beautiful virtues, where infidelity holds dominion with the sway of a despot, where virtue is trampled underfoot and vice carries off the prize of honor, where sins are drunk down like water, where the just behold so many foreshadowings of Hell and of abomination: retire from those lakes of wretchedness, divest yourselves of those sentiments of vanity, in order to go into a place where an everlasting springtime flourishes, and where the sad and horrible phantoms of misery are no longer to be witnessed.

Let us advance, then, dear souls, let us not be stayed by the enticements of the age. There is above us a solid, a permanent good, which inebriates souls with so sweet an ambrosia, that they can scarcely know their joys, so many contentments do they possess.

Are you not weary of seeing the rivers flow on to the sea, and the seasons of the year follow one another in invariable order? Are you not content with having gathered the flowers of spring, and tasted the fruits of autumn? Is it not enough to have bruised the roses and the lilies, with which to sprinkle the couch of your sensuality?

Does it not suffice to have so often seen the sun and moon, so many days and nights? Think you that the trees of the forest will produce other leaves, or that nature will yield something new? The twinkling lamps of heaven will send down no other light.

Quit the world, then, devout souls. And if you would wish to postpone the will of the Lord, at least be prepared for the appointments of Heaven on the matter. Have your conscience always in a good state, so as to render an account of your actions; imagine that the judgment of God is every hour over your head, so that only a little sigh is needed to conduct you to sentence; that a faint can overpower us, and put us in a state in which we can no longer even know ourselves. The flower which at morning unfolded itself has at evening passed and gone. Consider that death may meet you in the morning; or at evening, that you may sink to rest with the sun; that in the gardens of the world, under the rose and the lily, death is hidden like a serpent in the grass.

O my God, I will not give Thee my soul, for it is already a long time since Thou hast purchased it at the price of Thy blood, and Thou hast withdrawn it from the captivity of sin and death. Happy shall it be if Thou receive it, pardoning its faults.

O great God! Now is the time to render an account; the justice of Thy judgments makes me fear, but Thy infinite mercy makes me hope. I cast myself into Thy arms to implore pardon; I will cast myself at Thy feet, and water them with my tears; may the stream that flows from my eyes be a testimony to my repentance, that I may have the happiness, through Thy infinite goodness, to share in the effects of Thy mercy! *Amen.*[1]

---

1   "The goodness of God is not opposed to His justice; for if it takes His victims in one way, it returns them in another; instead of overthrowing them by vengeance, it overthrows them by humility; instead of crushing them by chastisement, it crushes them by contrition; and if justice requires to be satisfied by blood, goodness offers that of a God. Thus, far from being antagonists, they cheerfully shake hands. We should neither presume nor despair. Presume not, O sinners, because it is true that God takes vengeance; but abandon not yourselves to despair, because, if I may be allowed the expression, it is still more true that God forgives."—*Bossuet.*

CHAPTER SIXTEEN

HOW MUCH GOD LOVES THE
SAINTS, NOTWITHSTANDING THEIR
DEFECTS AND IMPERFECTIONS

TO EVERY man, however holy he may be, there
always remains some imperfection, because he has
been drawn from nothingness: so that we do no injury
to the saints when, in recounting their virtues, we relate
their sins and defects, but, on the contrary, those who
write their lives seem, for this reason, to do a great injury
to mankind by concealing the sins and imperfections of
the saints, under pretence of honoring them, not referring
to the commencement of their lives, for fear of diminishing the esteem of their sanctity. Oh, no, indeed, this is not
to act properly; but it is to wrong the saints and all posterity. All the great saints, when writing the lives of other
saints, have told us their faults and imperfections candidly,
and thought, as was right, that by this means they should

render as much service to God, and even to the saints, as by recounting their virtues. The great St. Jerome, writing the eulogy of his dear daughter St. Paula, tells her imperfections plainly and openly, condemning some of her actions himself with an admirable ingenuousness, always making truth and sincerity walk hand in hand, in the description of her virtues and her defects, knowing well that one would be useless without the other. For, beholding the defects of the saints while admiring their lives, we learn how great is the goodness of God, who forgave them, and we also learn to avoid the like, and to do penance for them, as the saints have done, in the same manner as we behold their virtues in order to imitate them.[1]

When persons of the world wish to praise those whom they love, they always relate their accomplishments, their virtues, and their excellent qualities, giving them all the titles which may render them more honorable, carefully hiding their sins and imperfections, and scrupulously forgetting everything that might make them appear mean or contemptible; but our holy Mother the Church acts in quite a different manner; for, though she singularly loves her children, nevertheless, when she wishes to praise and exalt them, she exactly relates the sins which they committed before their conversion, in order to render more honor

---

1 "There are some saints," says a great servant of God, an author very enlightened in spiritual things, M. Boudon, "there are some saints, who never cease to commit many faults, and sometimes even more than other persons who have only a very middling virtue; but still there is a great difference between these two classes of souls. For the one, although they have many imperfections, have none voluntarily, and they would rather die than commit the smallest fault with full advertence; they have a true intention, as St. Augustine says, to do everything to arrive at high sanctity and to practice heroic virtue. The others, though freer from faults, are far from possessing such a vigorous love."

and glory to the majesty of Him who sanctified them, showing forth resplendently His infinite mercy by which He raised them from their miseries and sins, loading them afterwards with His graces, and giving them His holy love, by means of which they arrived at the height of sanctity.

Certainly, our good Mother the Church, in writing or recounting the sins of the saints, has had no other intention unless to show us that she does not wish we should be astonished or put in pain about what we have been, or at the sins which we have committed, or at our present miseries, provided we have a firm and inviolable resolution to belong entirely to God, and generously to embrace perfection and all the means which may help us to advance in holy love, acting in such a manner that this resolution may be efficacious, and may produce fruits. Indeed, our miseries and weaknesses, however great they may be, ought not to discourage us, but ought rather to humble us and make us cast ourselves into the arms of the divine mercy, which will be so much the more glorified in us as our miseries are greater, if happily we rise from them: which we ought to hope to do by means of the grace of Our Lord.

The great St. Chrysostom, speaking of St. Paul, praises him most appropriately, and discourses of him with so much honor and esteem that it is a wonderful thing to see how he relates the virtues, the perfections, the excellences, the prerogatives, the graces with which God had adorned and enriched the soul of the holy Apostle; but afterwards, the same doctor, to show that all these gifts and graces proceeded, not from the saint, but from the infinite goodness of God, treats of his defects, and very exactly relates his sins

and imperfections. "Behold," he says, "this cruel persecu-
tor of the Church—God makes of him a vessel of election;
behold this great sinner—God changes him from a wolf
into a lamb; behold with how many graces God replenishes
this obstinate and ambitious man, making him so submissive that he uses these words: "Lord, what wilt Thou have
me to do?" And so humble that he calls himself the least of
the Apostles and the greatest of sinners, and so charitable
that he becomes all to all to gain all." "Who is sick," says
this great Apostle, "and I am not sick? Who is sad, and I
am not sad? Who is joyful, and I am not joyful? Who is
scandalized, and I am not on fire?" Assuredly the ancient
Fathers, who wrote the lives of saints, were exceedingly pre-
cise in relating their defects and sins, in order to exalt and
magnify so much the more the goodness of Our Lord, who
was pleased thus to glorify Himself in them, showing the
efficacy of His grace, by which they were converted.

CHAPTER SEVENTEEN

THE SWEET AND HAPPY
DEATH OF THE PREDESTINED

GOD having once drawn His faithful servants to Him, and taken their salvation under His protection, He does not quit them until He has guided them to their journey's end, and lodged them safe in Heaven;[1] having received great services from His saints, He usually gives them towards the close of their days some foretastes

---

1 Behold in what terms Bossuet renders an account of the edifying manner in which Henrietta of England received the Last Sacraments: "How far superior did she appear to those tepid Christians who imagine their death to be at hand when they prepare for Confession, who receive the holy Sacraments only by force! This lady sends for the priests before sending for the physicians. She asks herself for the Sacraments of the Church, with compunction for Penance, with fear and yet with confidence for the Eucharist, with a pious eagerness for the holy Unction of the dying. Far from being terrified, she wishes to receive this last Sacrament with consciousness; she listens to the explanation of those holy ceremonies, of those apostolic prayers, which, by a sort of divine charm, suspend the most violent sorrows, which cause death to be forgotten (*I have often seen it*) by those who hear them with faith; she follows them, she conforms herself to them, she peacefully presents her body to the sacred oil, or rather to the blood of Jesus Christ, which flows so abundantly with this precious liquor."

of the felicity of the future life, in order the better to dispose them to sigh for that infinite beatitude which awaits
them in Paradise, to disgust them with all terrestrial things,
and to make them banish from their hearts every unworthy
desire: so that, seeing they can neither sing nor hear the
divine praises in this world according to their liking, they
enter into extraordinary desires of being delivered from the
fetters of this life, to go into a place where God is perfectly
and supremely loved; and those desires, taking possession
of their hearts, become so powerful and so pressing in the
breasts of those sacred lovers, that they render their souls all
languishing and sick of love, until this holy passion rises to
such a degree that they sweetly die of it.

Thus the glorious and seraphic St. Francis, having been
for a long time weary of living, weary with the strong affection of praising God, at last, in his closing years, received
by a special revelation an assurance of his eternal salvation,
and being no longer able to contain his joy, and his ardent
desires taking every day new increase, his soul at length
burst from his body with a spring towards Heaven, pro-
nouncing these sacred words: "Draw my soul out of prison,
O Lord, that I may bless Thy holy name; the just expect me
until Thou givest me the desired rest." So it is with all the
saints, whose death is ever most precious, though it happens in diverse ways, according to the Providence of God;
for their spirit, like a celestial nightingale, shut up in the
cage of the body, in which it cannot sing with freedom the
divine benedictions, knows well that it would warble better and intone more joyfully its beautiful notes, if it could
only gain the free air to enjoy its liberty and the society of

the other songsters, among the gay and flourishing hills of the happy country; therefore, delivered from the cage of the body, withdrawn from its mortal prison, set free from slavery, it flies on high to Heaven to be united with the choirs of angels and saints, and to join with them in a sweet harmony of delicious canticles, singing, praising, and blessing forever the infinite mercy of God.

My God, how desirable is such a death! Oh, how lovely is the temple to which the souls of the saints fly! There the vaults re-echo with praise; and what a happiness belongs to those who dwell in the sacred abode where so many celestial musicians and divine choristers sing with a holy emulation of love the song of everlasting sweetness!

As soon as a soul enters Paradise, to make irrevocably its home and resting place there, in those sacred mansions and those holy and desirable tabernacles, God disposes it and strengthens it, by the excellent light of His glory, to be capable of beholding so sublime and so resplendent an object as the Divinity. "Divers," says Pliny, "who, seeking for precious stones, descend into the sea, take some oil in their mouths, in order that, pouring it out, they may enjoy more day to see in the waters through which they move." In like manner, the saints being plunged in the ocean of the divine essence, God sheds through their understanding a special light, which makes a sort of day to them in the abyss of light inaccessible, in order that, by the brightness of glory, they may behold the brightness of the Divinity.

All the blessed are perfectly happy, and have an inexpressible contentment to know that after having satiated all the desires of their hearts, and fully replenished their every capacity in the enjoyment of an infinite good, which is God, yet there still remain, in this infinity, infinite perfections to be seen, to be enjoyed, and to be possessed, which the Divine Majesty alone knows, It alone comprehending Itself.

Ah! How beautiful it is to see those happy citizens of Paradise, and truly great Princes of the Holy Empire, more invested on all sides by the ocean of the Divinity, than fishes are enclosed by the waves in the bosom of the sea, than birds as they fly are environed by the air, than stars enchased in the azure firmament are surrounded by the heavens! Oh! What felicity, to be more intimately united to God than light is to the purest crystal, than fire to the gold which shines like the sun in the crucible, than the soul to the body, than grace to the soul! Let him who can, explain the full rejoicing of the saints, which springs from the unreserved enjoyment of the sovereign uncreated good, which is fathomed only by abysses, measured only by immensity, bounded only by infinity, limited only by eternity, and comprehended only by the Divinity itself. Thence the perfect friends of God, now fully possessed, draw an extreme contentment, seeing themselves infinitely above all that they could have expected, loaded with honor, inebriated with the most pleasurable torrents of the house of God, true rendezvous of all holy and chaste delights, which the most high God of peace and of all consolation spreads continually to rejoice His faithful servants, satiating them to the full, yet without disgust for the meats of His divinely royal table, worthy of the most happy, the most illustrious, and the most glorious monarch! God, as a most loving father, is pleased thus to feast and entertain His true children, begotten of His grace and recognized by the glory which He shares with them: which He does in a manner infinitely admirable; for, from enjoyment springs desire, and in proportion as desire increases, the enjoyment increases, this without weariness and that without anguish, both with perfect pleasure and contentment. It is said that those who keep in their mouth a certain Scythian herb suffer neither hunger nor thirst, so deliciously are they sustained by it; in like manner when the will enjoys God, it reposes in Him with a sovereign complacency, and, nevertheless, it ceases not the motion of its desires, ardently desiring love, and loving desire infinitely.

Nightingales take so much pleasure in their song, according to Pliny, that sometimes for fifteen days and nights, they never cease to warble, vying always with one another to sing better; so that when they sing most melodiously, they experience the greatest complacency, and this increase of complacency leads them to still greater efforts, their complacency rising in such a manner with their song, and their song with their complacency, that many a time they are seen to die, and their throat is found burst with the force of singing. O God! How melodiously do those beautiful souls, who hold the first rank in Heaven, and who surpass the ordinary blessed as much as they exceeded them in merits and sanctity here on earth, chant the divine benedictions! In proportion as they praise God, they are pleased with praising Him, and in proportion as they are pleased with praising Him, they desire to praise Him yet better; and to content themselves, unable to wish any increase to

God, because He has infinitely more than they can desire,
or even think of, they desire at least that His name may be
praised, exalted, blessed, honored, and glorified more and
more, in Heaven and on earth, by men and angels!

Would to God that we could act thus, and that all
the faculties of our souls were as so many sacred tubes, on
which to sound the divine canticles of praise and jubilation!

Chapter Eighteen

Death of the Saint's Young Sister, Jeanne de Sales, in the Arms of Madame de Chantal

WELL now, my dear daughter, is it not reasonable that the will of God should be accomplished in what is not pleasing to us, as well as in what is pleasing to us? But I must hasten to tell you that my good mother drank the chalice with a truly Christian constancy; and her virtue, of which I had so good an opinion before, has greatly advanced in my esteem.

On Sunday morning, she sent for my brother the Canon, to come to her, and because she had seen him very sad, and all the other brothers too, the preceding evening, she began to say to him: "I have been dreaming the whole night that my daughter Jane [Jeanne] was dead. Tell me, I pray, is it true?" My brother, who expected that I should have arrived to tell her, seeing this beautiful opportunity to make the announcement: "It is true, mother," he said. And nothing more; for he had not strength to add anything. "The will of God be done," said my good mother, and she wept for a time abundantly; and then, calling her maid: "I wish to rise," said she, "to go into the chapel, to pray to God for my poor daughter," and immediately she did as she had said. Not a single word of impatience, not a look of uneasiness, a thousand benedictions to God, and a thousand resignations to His will. Never have I seen a more tranquil sorrow: so many tears as were marvelous, yet all with the most simple emotions of the heart, without any kind of bitterness: she was still her dear child. Well now! Ought I not to love such a mother?

Yesterday, the Feast of All Saints, I was the extraordinary confessor to the family, and, with the Most Holy Sacrament, I sealed this mother's heart against all sadness. As for the rest, she thanks you infinitely for the care and the maternal love you exercised in regard to the little deceased, with a gratitude as great as if God had preserved her by this means. The same is said to you by all the members of the family, which has shown itself extremely well pleased with the circumstances of this death; above all, our Boisy— whom I love especially.

I know well that you would fain ask me: "And you, how did you bear it?" Yes, for you desire to know what I did. Alas! My daughter, I am only a man, and nothing more: my heart was affected more than I ever could have imagined. But the truth is, the grief of my mother, and yours, contributed much to it; for I was afraid of your heart, and my mother's. But, Live Jesus! I will always take the side of Divine Providence; it does everything well, and disposes of all things for the best. What a happiness for this child, to have been *taken away from the world, that iniquity might not alter her understanding,* and to have left this miry place before being defiled by it! We gather the strawberries and the cherries before the bergamot pears; but it is because their season requires it. Let us allow God to gather what He has planted in His orchard: He takes everything in its season.

You can imagine, my dear daughter, how cordially I loved this little sister. I had begotten her to her Saviour; it was I who baptized her with my own hand: now about fourteen years ago. She was the first creature on whom I exercised my sacerdotal powers. I was her spiritual father, and fondly promised myself to make of her one day something good. And that which rendered her exceedingly dear to me (I speak the truth), was that she was yours. But, nevertheless, my dear daughter, in the midst of my heart of flesh, which has experienced so many emotions at this death, I perceive very clearly a certain tranquility, a certain sweet repose of my mind on Divine Providence, which spreads through my soul a great contentment, blended with its grief.

You have now my feelings represented to you as I have been able. But you, my dear daughter, what would you say, when you would tell me how you found yourself on this occasion? Tell me, I pray, does not our mariner's needle always point to its beautiful star, to its holy star, to its God? Your heart, what did it do? Did you scandalize those who saw you on this event? Now, my daughter, tell me this plainly; for, you see, I would not be content if you offered your life, or that of any of your other children, in exchange for that of the deceased.

No, my dear daughter, we must not only be willing that God should strike us, but we must be glad that it should be on the side He pleases. We must leave the choice to God, for it belongs to Him. David offered his life for that of his Absalom, but it was for fear his son should have died lost: in this case we must conjure God; but in temporal losses, O my daughter, let God slap us and pinch us wherever He pleases; and whatever chords of our lute He pleases to touch, let Him always find a sweet harmony. Lord Jesus! Without reserve, without *ifs,* without *buts,* without exception, without limitation, may Thy will be done over father, over mother, over daughter, in everything, and everywhere. Ah! I do not say that we must not desire or pray for their preservation; but to say to God: Leave this one and take that one—my dear daughter, we must not say it. Neither shall we say it, my daughter; no, by the help of divine grace.

It seems to me that I see you, my dear daughter, with your vigorous heart, which loves and desires ardently. I am pleased with it; for those hearts half-dead-and-alive—to what are they good? But we must have a particular exercise, once every week, namely, to desire and love the will of God more earnestly, more tenderly, and more affectionately than anything in the world, and this, not only in occurrences that are supportable, but even in those most insupportable. You will find something exquisite on this point in the little book, the *Spiritual Combat,* which I have so often recommended to you.

Alas! My daughter, to speak the truth, this lesson is high; but God, for whom we learn it, is the Most High. You have, my daughter, four children; you have a father, a father-in-law, a dear brother, and then, again, a spiritual father: all these are very dear to you, and with reason, for God wishes it. Well! If God were to take them all from you, would you not still have enough in having Him? Is not this according to your view! When we have only God, have we not abundance?

Alas! The Son of God, our dear Jesus, had scarcely so much on the cross, when, having quitted and left all for obedience to His Father, He was abandoned and forsaken by His Father; and the torrent of anguish carrying away His barque to desolation, scarcely could He recognize the needle of the compass, which was not only turned to, but was inseparably united with, His Father. Yes, He was *one* with His Father; but the inferior part neither knew nor perceived it: a trial which the divine goodness never made, and never will make, on any other soul; for no one could endure it.

My daughter, though God takes everything away from us, yet He will never take Himself away, so long as we do not wish it. But still more: all our losses and separations are only for a little moment. Oh, truly, for so little we ought to have patience.

I pour myself out, it seems, a little too much. But what! I am my heart, which never thinks it says too much with so dear a daughter as you. I send you an "escutcheon," to please you, and since you desire to have the services performed in the place where this child reposes in her body,

I am satisfied, but without great pomp, unless that which
the Christian custom justly requires; for to what good is
anything else? You will have drawn out afterwards in a list
all the expenses, and those of her sickness, and you will
send the account to me; for I wish this also. And in the
meanwhile, we will pray to God on our side for her soul,
and pleasantly offer her little honors. We will not meet at
her month's mind;[1] no, my daughter, there is no need for so
much ceremony about one who never held any rank in the
world; for it would rather be to mock her. You know me; I
love simplicity in death and in life. I shall be glad to know
the name and title of the church where she reposes.

_____
1   Month's mind—a Requiem Mass offered one month after a person's death.—*Publisher*, 2013.

CHAPTER NINETEEN

DEATH OF THE COUNTESS DE SALES, MOTHER OF THE SAINT[1]

B UT, O my God! My dearest daughter, should we not in all things, and everywhere, adore the Supreme Providence, whose counsels are always holy, good and amiable? Behold how He has been pleased to draw from this miserable world, our dearest and most excellent mother, to have her, as I confidently hope, near Himself, and at His right hand. Let us confess, my well-beloved daughter, let us confess, *that God is good and His mercy endureth forever;* all His *wills* are *just,* and all His *decrees equitable;* His *good plea-sure* is always *holy,* and His ordinances are most amiable.

As for me, I confess, my daughter, that I experienced great grief on this separation; for I must make the confession of my weakness, after having made that of the Divine Goodness. But nevertheless, my daughter, it was a tranquil

---

1 Letter to Madame de Chantal [St. Jane Frances de Chantal].

grief, though acute, for I said with David: "I have been
silent, O Lord, and opened not my mouth, because Thou
hast done it." Had it not been for this, I would undoubtedly have cried out piteously under the stroke; but it was
not according to my mind, that I should dare to do so,
or manifest any discontent under the strokes of a paternal hand, which, in truth, thanks to its goodness, I have
learned to love tenderly from my youth.

But you would wish perhaps to know how this good
woman ended her days. Behold then a little history of it;
for it is to you I speak, to you, I say, to whom I have given
this mother's place in my memento at Mass, without taking away that which you had before; for I could not bring
myself to do it, so firmly do you hold that which you
hold in my heart, and thus you hold the first and the last
place there.

This mother then came here in winter; and during the
month which she remained, she made a general review of
her soul, and renewed her desires of well-doing, with very
great affection indeed, and she went away the most con-
tented in the world with me, from whom, as she said, she
had drawn more consolation than she had ever done before.
She continued in this good way until Ash Wednesday,
when she went to the parish church of Torens, where she
confessed and communicated with very great devotion, and
heard three Masses and vespers. During the day, being in
bed, and unable to sleep, she caused her maid to read her
three chapters of *The Introduction,* to entertain her in good
thoughts, and desired her to mark the *protestation* to be
made the following morning; but God was content with

her good will, and disposed of matters otherwise: for morning being come, this good lady arose, and, while combing her hair, suddenly she fell down as if dead.

My poor brother, your child, who still slept, being informed of what had happened, ran in his night-dress, and lifted her up, and helped her to walk, and assisted her with "essences," "imperial waters," and other things which are recommended in cases of accidents; so that she recovered, and began to speak, but almost unintelligibly, so much had the tongue and the throat been affected.

A messenger came for me, and I hastened immediately with the physician and the apothecary, who found her apoplectic, and paralyzed in one half the body. Her stupor was of such a nature, that it was easy to awake her; and during those moments of consciousness, she manifested a perfect clearness of judgment, using the hand that still remained sound, and speaking very apropos of God and her soul. Sometimes she sought for the crucifix, groping (so suddenly had she become blind), and kissed it. Never did she take anything without making the sacred sign over it: and thus she received the holy oils.

On my arrival, blind and drowsy as she was, she caressed me much, and said: "This is my son and my father," and kissed me, embracing me with her arm, and kissed the hand to me before everything. She continued in the same state nearly two days and a half, after which it was difficult to awake her; and on the first of March, she surrendered her soul sweetly and peacefully to Our Lord, with a countenance of greater beauty than perhaps she had ever borne in life, remaining one of the loveliest dead I have ever seen.

I have still to tell you that I had the courage to give her the last benediction, to close her eyes and mouth, and to give her the kiss of peace, at the moment of her departure: after which my heart filled, and I wept over this mother more than I have ever done since I entered the Church; but it was without spiritual bitterness, thanks be to God! Behold what passed.

Chapter Twenty

The Rapidity of Time

THESE temporal years pass away; the months are reduced to weeks, the weeks to days, the days to hours, and the hours to moments, which are all that we possess, but which we possess only in proportion as they perish. The more perishable our existence, the more amiable ought it to be to us, since this life being full of miseries, we should have no greater consolation than to know that it rapidly vanishes to give place to a holy eternity, which is prepared for us in the abundance of the mercy of God, and to which our soul incessantly aspires by continual thoughts arising from its own nature, though it cannot hope to arrive there but by other thoughts more exalted, with which the Author of nature inspires us.

Indeed, I never consider eternity without much sweetness; for, I say, how can my soul extend its thought to this infinity, unless there is some kind of proportion between it and eternity? But when I feel that my desire runs after my thought, my joy takes an incredible increase; for, I know that we never desire, with a true desire, anything but what is possible. My desire then assures me that I can possess eternity: what remains to me more than to hope that I shall possess it? And this assurance proceeds from the knowledge I have of the infinite goodness of Him, who would not create souls capable of thinking on, and tending to, eternity, without giving them the means of attaining to it.

Let us then often say: Everything passes, and after the few days of this mortal life, an infinite eternity will come. Little does it matter whether we have conveniences or inconveniences here, provided that for all eternity we are happy.

A great soul sends all its best thoughts and affections forward to the infinity of eternity, and being immortal, it esteems too short all that which is not eternal, too small all that which is not infinite, and rising about the delights, or rather the vile amusements, of this life, it keeps its eyes steadily fixed on the immensity of eternal goods, and the vastness of eternal years.[1]

Oh, how desirable is eternity, at the cost of miserable and perishable vicissitudes! Let time flow by, with which we flow on to be transformed into the glory of the children of God.

---

1   An author of the present day, rather original, writes these lines: "Come, die in peace; have you not for a long time been dying a little every day? Death has nothing to surprise you; meet it like an old friend. You are an exile, it comes to lead you back to your country; you are a martyr, it brings you the palm of victory.

"What thread remains to be broken? None, but that of your life. Your balloon is impatient; it has only to throw out the sand, and presently it is aloft, between the eagles and the sun."

Alas! When I consider how I have employed God's time, I am in pain lest He should not give me His eternity, since He gives it only to those who use His time well.

O God! The years pass away, and run as a thread imperceptibly one after another; dividing our existence, they divide our mortal life, and ending, they end our days.

Oh, how incomparably more amiable is eternity, since its duration is without end, and its days are without nights, and its contentments are without variation! How much I desire that, in a high degree, you may possess this admirable good of a holy eternity! What a happiness for my soul, if God, showing it mercy, grants it also this consolation!

CHAPTER TWENTY-ONE

WE SHOULD ABANDON OURSELVES TO GOD IN LIFE AND IN DEATH

A MONG the praises given by the saints to Abraham, St. Paul mentions this above every other, *that he believed, hoping against all hope.* God had promised to multiply his posterity as the stars of heaven, and as the sand of the seashore; and, notwithstanding, gave him an order to sacrifice his only son. Yet Abraham did not lose hope, but believed that while obeying the commandment to immolate his son, God would not fail to keep His word.

Great indeed was his hope; for he saw nothing on which to rely, except the word of God. Oh, how true and solid a foundation is this word, for it is infallible!

Abraham proceeded then with extraordinary simplicity to fulfill the directions of God; for he made no more hesitation or reply than when God had told him to quit his country and his father's house. Walking three days and three nights with his son, not knowing precisely whither he went, carrying the wood of sacrifice, his son asked him where was the holocaust, to which he replied: "My son, the Lord will provide it."

O my God! How happy we should be, if we could accustom ourselves to make answer to our hearts, when they are in fretfulness about anything: *Our Lord will provide for it,* and then to have no more anxiety or trouble than Isaac! For he was silent afterwards, believing that the Lord would provide what was necessary, as his father had told him.

Great indeed is the confidence which God requires we should have in His paternal care and in His holy Providence; but why should we not have it, seeing that no person was ever deceived therein, and no one confides in God without reaping the fruits of his confidence?

Consider what Our Lord says to His Apostles, to establish them in this holy and loving confidence: "When I sent you into the world without purse, without silver, without any provision, was anything wanting to you?" They say: "No. Go." He says to them, "And be not solicitous for what you shall eat, or what you shall drink, or how you shall be clothed, or how you shall speak when brought before magistrates; for, on every occasion, My Father who is in Heaven, will give you that which is necessary."

"But I am so little spiritual," someone will say. "I do not know how to treat with the great, I have no knowledge." It is all one; go, and confide in God, for He says: "Though a mother should forget her child, yet will not I forget you; for, I bear you engraven on My heart, and on My hands."

Think you that He who is careful to provide nourishment for the birds of the air and the beasts of the field, that neither sow nor reap, will fail to provide all that is necessary for those who fully trust in His Providence, and who are capable of being forever united with Him, who is the sovereign good?[1]

We ought to know that to leave oneself, is nothing else than to quit one's own will, in order to give it to God; for it will avail us little to renounce ourselves, unless we unite ourselves to the divine goodness: to act otherwise, would be to imitate those philosophers who made admirable abandonments of all things and of themselves, but only under some vain pretence of philosophy. Witness Epictetus, who, being a slave by condition, and his master wishing to set him free on account of his great wisdom, would not accept his liberty, one of the greatest blessings, but remained as he was in slavery, so poor, that at his death he left only a lamp, which sold exceedingly dear, having belonged to so great a man.

As for us, let us not seek to abandon ourselves, unless to leave ourselves at the disposal of the will of God. There are many, who say to Our Lord: "I give myself entirely to Thee, without any reserve"; but there are few who embrace the practice of this renunciation, which is nothing else than

---

1 "From the largest creatures even to the least, the Providence of God is everywhere apparent; it feeds the little birds who invoke it from the break of day by the melody of their songs; and those flowers whose beauty so quickly fades away, it decks more superbly during the brief moment of their existence, than Solomon was arrayed in all his glory. Can you, O men, whom He has made to His image, whom He has enlightened with His knowledge, whom He has called to His Kingdom, imagine that He forgets you, and that you are the only creatures on which the ever vigilant eyes of His paternal Providence are not opened? Are not you of much more value than they?"—*Bossuet.*

a perfect submission in receiving all kinds of events, according as they happen, by the order of God's Providence, as well affliction as consolation, sickness as health, poverty as riches, contempt as honor, opprobrium as glory.

I speak of the superior part of the soul; for there is no doubt but that the inferior part, the natural inclination, tends always more to the side of honor than to that of contempt, to the side of riches rather than to that of poverty, although no one is ignorant that contempt and poverty are more agreeable to God than honor and abundance.[2]

Let us live as long as God pleases in this valley of tears, with an entire submission to His holy will. I considered the other day what authors write concerning halcyons, little birds that poise on the roadstead of the sea. It is, that they make their nests round, and so closely pressed together, that the water cannot at all penetrate them, and there is only one little hole in the top by which they can breathe. Within they lodge their little ones, so that the sea surprising them, they float securely on the surface of the waves, without being filled or submerged, and the air entering by the little hole serves so nicely to balance these little chicklings and their little skiffs that they are never capsized. Oh! How I desire that our hearts should be thus closely pressed

---

2 "Full of confidence in that vast extensive Providence, which embraces all causes and all effects in its designs, the Christian is replenished with joy, and learns to turn all things to good. If God sends him prosperity, he accepts with submission the present from Heaven, and honors that mercy which delights in bestowing favors on the miserable. If adversity, he remembers that 'trial produces hope,' that war is made to secure peace, and that if his virtue conquers, it will one day be crowned. Never does he despair, because he is never without resource; can he despair of his fortunes to whom there still remains an entire kingdom, and a kingdom no other than that of God? What power can cast him down, who is supported by so sweet a hope."—*Bossuet.*

together, every chink stopped up, so that if the torments and tempests of the world seize upon them, they may not penetrate them, and that there should be only one opening, on the side of Heaven, by which to breathe to our Saviour! And this nest: for what should it serve? For the little fledglings of its Maker, for divine and celestial affections. But while the halcyons are building their nests, and their little ones are yet too tender to endure the shocks of the billows, ah! God has care of them, and looks down on them with pity, preventing the sea from overturning and destroying them. O God! This sovereign goodness will also secure the nest of our hearts, on account of its holy love, against all the assaults of the world, or will preserve us from being assailed by them. Ah, how much I love those birds, which are surrounded by water, live on the air, and see only heaven! They swim like fishes, and sing like birds; and that which pleases me most is, that their anchor is cast on the upper side, and not on the lower, to steady them against the waves. May the sweet Jesus vouchsafe to form us so, that though environed by the world and the flesh, we may live by the spirit; that, in the midst of the vanities of the world, we may always look to Heaven; that, dwelling amongst men, we may associate with angels; and that the foundation of our hopes may be on high in Paradise. Let holy love be always and everywhere our chief love. Alas, when will it consume our life, and make us die to ourselves, to live only to our Saviour? To Him alone belong honor, glory, and benediction forever! Since our inviolable purpose, and invariable resolution, tends continually to the love of God, never are words of the love of God out of place.

I shall say nothing further to you, either on the great abandonment of ourselves and of all things to God, or on the departure from our country and the house of our parents. No, I do not wish to speak of them. May God be pleased to enlighten us, and to show us His good pleasure; for at the risk of all that is in us, we shall follow Him into whatever place He leads us. Oh, how good it is to be with Him, no matter where!

I think on the soul of the good thief. Our Lord had said that it would that day be with Him in paradise, and no sooner was it separated from its body than it passed down to hell. Yes, for it would be with Our Lord, as Our Lord descended into Hell.[3] It went thither then with Him. O God! What did it think on, while descending and beholding those abysses before its interior eyes? I believe it said with Job: "Who will grant me, O my God, that Thou mayest defend and preserve me in hell?" And with David: "No, I shall fear no evil; for the Lord is with me."

So long as our resolutions live, I shall be untroubled. Though we die, though everything be overthrown, it matters little, provided they subsist.

The nights are days when God is in our heart, and the days are nights when He is absent.

---

3   The hell into which Our Lord descended was the "Limbo of the Fathers," where the souls of the just from the Old Testament were awaiting the Redemption.—*Publisher,* 2013.

OF ST. FRANCIS DE SALES TO THE PIOUS READER

IT IS with all my heart, I say the word, "Adieu." To God (*A Dieu*) may you ever belong in this life, serving Him faithfully in the midst of the pains we all have in carrying our crosses, and in the immortal life, blessing Him eternally with all the celestial court. The greater good of our souls is to be with God; and the greatest good, to be with God alone.

He who is with God alone, is never sad, unless for having offended God, and his sadness then consists in a profound but tranquil and peaceful humility and submission, after which he rises again in the Divine Goodness, by a sweet and perfect confidence, without chagrin or vexation.

He who is with God alone seeks only God, and because God is no less in tribulation than in prosperity, he remains in peace during times of adversity.

He who is with God alone thinks often of Him in the midst of the occupations of this life.

He who is with God alone would be glad that everyone should know he wishes to serve God, and to be engaged in exercises suitable to keep him united to God.

Live then entirely to God; desire only to please Him, and to please creatures only in Him, and for Him. What greater blessing can I wish you? Thus, then, by this continual wish I make for your soul, I say: Adieu.

To God let us belong, without end, without reserve, without measure, as He is ours forever. May we always unite our little crosses with His great one!

To God let us live, and to God without anything more, since out of Him, and without Him, we seek for nothing: no, not even for ourselves, who, indeed, out of Him, and without Him, are only true nothings.

Adieu. I desire for you the abundance of Divine Love, which is and will be forever the only good of our hearts, given to us only for Him, who has given His Heart entirely to us.

Let Jesus be our crown! Let Mary be our hope! I am, in the name of the Son and the Mother,

Sincerely yours,

Francis de Sales

Supplement

1. We Should Not Despair of the Salvation of Any Sinner[1]

ST. FRANCIS de Sales, says the Bishop of Belley, never wished that the repentance of any sinner should be despaired of before his last breath, observing that this life was the way of our pilgrimage, in which those who walked might fall, and those who fell might, by grace, rise again, and, like the giants in the fable, they sometimes rose stronger than they had fallen, grace superabounding where sin had abounded.

He went still further; for, even after death, he did not wish that anyone should pass a bad judgment on those who had led a bad life, unless it regarded those of whose damnation we are assured by the truth of the Holy Scripture. Beyond this point, He would not allow anyone to seek to penetrate into the secrets of God, which are reserved to His wisdom.

---

1   We take this chapter from the *Spirit of St. Francis de Sales*, by Camus [Bishop of Belley].

His principal reason was, that, as the first grace of justification does not fall under the merit of any preceding work, so the last grace, which is that of final perseverance, is not given to any merit either. Besides, who has known the mind of the Lord, and who has been His counselor? For this reason, He wished that, even after the last breath, we should hope well of the deceased person, however sad an end he might have seemed to make, because we can only form very uncertain conjectures, founded on external appearances, in which the most experienced are often deceived.[2]

2. Sentiments of St. Francis de Sales on the Number of the Elect

The extreme gentleness of St. Francis de Sales, says the Bishop of Belley, from whom we borrow this chapter, always led him to the mildest opinions, however little probability they carried. We were conversing one day, in company, on this dreadful word of the Gospel: "Many are called, but few are chosen." Someone remarked that the number of the elect was called a little flock, as that of fools, or of the reprobate, was called infinite, and such things. He answered that he thought very few Christians (he spoke of those in the true Church, out of which there is no salvation) would be damned; because, he said, having the root of the True Faith, sooner or later it usually yields its fruit,

---

2   We read the following passage in the *Life of Père De Ravignan:* "In certain deaths there are hidden mysteries of mercy and strokes of grace, in which the eye of man beholds only the strokes of justice. By the gleams of the last light, God reveals Himself to souls whose greatest misfortune was to have been ignorant of Him; and the last sigh, understood by Him who searches hearts, may be a groan that asks for pardon."

which is salvation, and from being dead, becomes living by charity.

And when asked what, then, was the meaning of this word of the Gospel concerning the small number of the elect, he said that in comparison with the rest of the world and with infidel nations, the number of Christians was very small, but that of this small number there would be very few lost, according to this remarkable sentence: "There is no damnation for those who are in Jesus Christ." (*Rom.* 8:1). Which, indeed, is to be understood of justifying grace;[3] but this grace is not separated from a faith living and animated by charity. Moreover, as He who gives the grace to begin, gives also the grace to perfect the undertaking, so it is credible that the vocation to Christianity, which is a work of God, is a perfect work, and conducts to the end of all consummation, which is glory.

I added another reason, and he was pleased with it: that the mercy of God being above all His works, and swimming over His justice, as oil over vinegar, there was every reason for trusting in His own natural disposition to pity and forgive, abundantly shown forth in the copious redemption of the Saviour; and there was no sign for believing that God would have commenced to erect the salvation of the true Christian by faith, which is its foundation, without proceeding with it to the end, which consists in charity.

This doctrine is of great consolation, provided it does not make us negligent in doing good; for, it is not enough to say with the ancients: *The temple of the Lord, the temple*

---

3 Justifying grace—that is, Sanctifying Grace.—*Publisher,* 2013.

of the Lord—the Church, the Church, I am in the bosom of the true Church. Since the Church is holy, and the pillar of truth, it is our duty to live holily, as well as to believe truly; for, to commit crimes in the house of God, is to defile His sanctuary, and to render oneself doubly guilty. And who is unaware that the servant who knew the will of his Master, and did not trouble himself to perform it, deserved a double chastisement?

We should fear, said St. Francis de Sales, the judgments of God, but without discouragement, and take courage at the sight of His mercies, but without presumption. Those who have an excessive and inordinate fear of being damned show plainly that they have great need of humility and submission. We must indeed abase, annihilate, lose ourselves, but this ought to be to gain, preserve, save ourselves. That humility which is prejudicial to charity, is assuredly a false humility. Such is that which leads to trouble, to discouragement, to despair; for it is contrary to charity, which, while commanding us *to work out our salvation with fear and trembling,* forbids us at the same time to diffide in the goodness of God, who desires the conversion and salvation of all.

3. The Souls in Purgatory

The opinion of St. Francis de Sales, says the Bishop of Belley, was that, from the thought of Purgatory, we should draw more consolation than pain. The greater number of those, he said, who fear Purgatory so much, do so in consideration of their own interests, and of the love they bear themselves rather than the interests of God, and this happens because those who treat of this place from the pulpit usually speak of its pains, and are silent of the happiness and peace which are found in it.

No doubt the torments are so great that the greatest sufferings of this life cannot be compared with them; but still, the interior satisfaction there is such, that no enjoyment or prosperity on earth can equal it.

The souls in Purgatory are in a constant state of union with God.

They are perfectly submissive to His will, or, to speak better, their will is so transformed into the will of God, that they cannot wish for anything but what God wishes; in such a manner, that if Paradise were opened to them, they would rather precipitate themselves into Hell than appear before God with the stains which they still perceive on themselves.

They are purified voluntarily and lovingly, because such is the divine good pleasure. The souls in Purgatory are there indeed for their sins, sins which they have detested, and sovereignly detested; but as to the abjection and pain that still remain, of being detained there, and deprived for a time of the joy of the blessed in Paradise, they endure all that lovingly, and devoutly pronounce this canticle of the divine justice: "Thou art just, O Lord, and thy judgment is right."

They wish to be there in the manner that pleases God, and for as long a time as He pleases.

They are impeccable, and cannot have the least motion of impatience, or be guilty of the smallest imperfection.

They love God more than themselves, and more than

all things else, with a perfect, pure, and disinterested love.

They are consoled by angels.

They are assured of their salvation.

Their most bitter bitterness is in the most profound peace.

If Purgatory is a kind of Hell as regards pain, it is a kind of Paradise as regards the sweetness which charity diffuses through the heart—charity which is stronger than death, and more powerful than Hell, and whose lamps are fire and flames.

A state more desirable than terrible, since its flames are flames of love.

Terrible, nevertheless, since they postpone the end of all consummation, which consists in seeing and loving God, and in this vision and love, to praise and glorify Him for all eternity. With regard to this subject, St. Francis de Sales approved very much of the admirable *Treatise on Purgatory*, written by the blessed Catherine of Genoa.

If these things be so, I shall be asked, why recommend so much the souls in Purgatory to our charity?

The reason is, because, notwithstanding their advantages, the state of these souls is still very sad and truly deserving of compassion, and, moreover, the glory which they will render to God in Heaven is delayed. These two motives ought to engage us, by our prayers, our fasts, our alms, and all kinds of good works, especially by offering the Holy Sacrifice of the Mass for them, to procure their speedy deliverance.

When any of St. Francis de Sales' friends or acquaintances died, he never grew weary of speaking fondly of them, or recommending them to the prayers of others.

His usual expression was: "We do not remember sufficiently our dead, our faithful departed;" and the proof of it is, that we do not speak enough of them. We turn away from that discourse as from a sad subject, we leave the dead to bury their dead; their memory perishes from us with the sound of their mourning bell; we forget that the friendship which ends, even with death, is never true, Holy Scripture assuring us that true love is stronger than death.

He was accustomed to say that in this single work of mercy, the thirteen others are assembled.

Is it not, he said, in some manner, to visit the sick, to obtain by our prayers the relief of the poor suffering souls in Purgatory?

Is it not to give drink to those who thirst after the vision of God, and who are enveloped in burning flames, to share with them the dew of our prayers?

Is it not to feed the hungry, to aid in their deliverance by the means which faith suggests?

Is it not truly to ransom prisoners?

Is it not to clothe the naked, to procure for them a garment of light, a raiment of glory?

Is it not an admirable degree of hospitality, to procure their admission into the heavenly Jerusalem, and to make them fellow citizens with the saints and domestics of God?

Is it not a greater service to place souls in Heaven, than to bury bodies in the earth?

As to spirituals, is it not a work whose merit may be compared to that of counseling the weak, correcting the wayward, instructing the ignorant, forgiving offences, enduring injuries? And what consolation, however great, that can be given to the afflicted of this world, is comparable with that which is brought by our prayers, to those poor souls who have such bitter need of them?

4. MOTIVES ON ACCOUNT OF WHICH IMPERFECT CHRISTIANS OUGHT NOT TO FEAR THEIR PASSAGE TO ETERNITY, AND MAY EVEN DESIRE IT [4]

As the Christian life is only an imitation and expression of the life which Jesus Christ led for us, so the Christian death ought to be only an imitation and expression of the death which Jesus Christ endured for us. Jesus Christ died to satisfy the justice of God for the sins of all men, and to put an end to the reign of iniquity, to render to His Father the most perfect obedience, by submitting to the sentence of death justly pronounced against all sinners, whose place He held, to render by His death an infinite homage to the majesty of God, and to acknowledge His sovereign dominion over all creatures. Every Christian is obliged to accept death in these same dispositions, and should esteem himself only too happy in the thought that Jesus Christ wished to unite the Sacrifice of His divine life, infinitely more precious than the lives of all men and angels, with the sacrifice which each one of us should make to God of our miserable and unworthy life, and that He wished to render our death,

---

4   We have so often met, in the exercise of our holy ministry, with souls who have an excessive fear of death, that we have thought it a duty to add to the consoling reflections of St. Francis de Sales another chapter, the most solid we know on the subject. [This note and this section appear to have been written by Fr. Huguet, the compiler.—*Publisher*, 2013.]

by uniting it with His, capable of meriting for us an eternal life. To die without participating in these dispositions of Jesus Christ at death, is not to die as a Christian, it is to die of necessity as a beast, it is to die as the reprobate.[5]

Every Christian is obliged to labor for the acquisition of these dispositions during his whole life, which is only given him to learn how to die well. We should often adore in Jesus Christ that ardent zeal which He had to satisfy the justice of God and to destroy sin, that spirit of obedience and sacrifice in which He lived and died, and which He still retains in the mystery of the Eucharist. We should ask Him to share it with us, especially during the time of the Holy Sacrifice of the Mass and Communion, when Jesus Christ offers Himself again to His Father in these same dispositions, and comes to us to communicate them to us. The more we participate in these holy dispositions, the less we shall fear a death which ought to be most precious and meritorious before God, and which will be the more so, as we shall more fully enter into the designs of Jesus Christ, who, dying really but once, to render to His Father the supreme honor which was due to Him, desired to offer to Him till the end of ages the death of each of His members, as a continuation of His sacrifice.

One of the chief effects of the Incarnation and death of Jesus Christ has been to deliver us from the fear of death: He became man, and a mortal man, *that He might destroy by His death him who was the prince of death, that is to say, the devil, and that He might deliver those whom the fear of*

---

5 A Christian would implicitly participate in these dispositions simply by being in the state of grace.—*Publisher,* 2013.

death held in continual servitude during life. Is it not in some manner to dishonor the victory of Jesus Christ over death, to tremble before an enemy whom He has vanquished, and to remain still in slavery through fear of dying?

Jesus Christ ardently desired the arrival of the hour that would consummate His sacrifice, by the effusion of His blood: "I have a baptism," so He calls His Passion, "Wherewith I am to be baptized, and how am I straitened until it be accomplished!" Should not a Christian, who has the honor of being one of His members, enter into His spirit, and desire the accomplishment of the baptism with which he is to be baptized? For death ought to appear to the true Christian as a baptism, in which he is to be washed from all his sins, and regenerated to a life of immortality, perfectly exempt from every corruption of sin. We should, then, like Jesus, desire with ardor to sacrifice our life as soon as possible: firstly, to render to the sovereign majesty of God, and all His divine perfections, the greatest glory that any creature can render to Him, and to render the most perfect homage to the death of Jesus Christ, our God and Saviour; secondly, to offer to God the most worthy thanksgiving, in gratitude for having sacrificed for us the life of His Son on the cross, as well as for having continued during so many ages to immolate His Body and Blood on our altars, and in gratitude for having given us His Holy Spirit and the life of grace, which is more precious than all the lives in the world; thirdly, to offer to God the fullest satisfaction that we are able to offer Him for our sins, by offering Him our death in union with that of Jesus Christ; fourthly, to draw down upon ourselves the greatest mercies of God, by an humble acceptance of death, and by the continual sacrifice which we shall make to Him of our life. For, although our life is so vile a thing, so little worthy of being offered to God in sacrifice, defiled as it is with so many sins, yet it is the most considerable present we can make to Him; and God is so good as to receive this remnant of sin, as a sacrifice of sweet odor.

A countless number of martyrs, of every age, sex, and country, have run to death with joy, and looked upon it as their greatest happiness to be able to sacrifice themselves for God in the midst of the most dreadful torments. The pagan or irregular life which some among them had led previously did not stay their ardor; because they hoped by their death entirely to repair the past. "Why," says St. Jerome, "do we not imitate them in something?" Are we not, like them, the disciples of a God crucified for our salvation, and destined to the same kingdom of Heaven? It is true that we have not, like them, the happiness of offering to God a bloody death; but, why should we not endeavor to supply its place, by the continual oblation that we can make to Him of the kind of death which He destines for us? "For I venture to say," adds this holy father, "that there is as much, and perhaps more, merit in offering to Him our life during the successive moments in which He preserves it to us, than in losing it once by the cruelty of executioners. The sacrifice which we make to God of our life, if sincere, is the greatest act of love that we can make." St. Augustine says: "If the angels could envy any privilege in man, it is his ability to die for the love of God."

We ask of God every day that His kingdom should

come. This kingdom of God will be perfectly established in us only by death, which will be for each of us an end to sin, the destruction of concupiscence, and the beginning of the absolute reign of justice and charity. To ask of God, every day, the coming of His kingdom, and, at the same time, to fear death excessively—are these things easily allied? The desire of the kingdom of God and of eternal life is essential to salvation. "It is not sufficient," says St. Augustine, "to believe by faith in a blessed life, we must love it by charity, and wish that we were already in the celestial abode; and it is impossible to have these dispositions in the heart, without being glad to depart from this life." At the commencement of the divine prayer in which we ask of God the coming of His kingdom, He orders us to say to Him: "Our Father, Who art in Heaven." If we sincerely believe that God is our Father, and we His children, how can we fear to go to our Heavenly Father, in order to reign with Him, to enjoy His possessions, and to repose forever on His bosom?

The Scripture represents all the faithful as so many persons who expect the last coming of Jesus Christ, who love His coming, and who go forward to meet Him as far as lies in them by their groans and desires. Why are we Christians? Why are we converted to God? "It is," says St. Paul, "To serve the true and living God, and to expect the Heaven of His Son Jesus, whom He has raised up, and who has delivered us from the wrath to come." To whom will the Lord, *as a just judge, render the crown of justice on the great day?* The same Apostle answers, that it will be *to those who love His coming. Since the earth, and all that it contains, must be consumed by fire,* which will precede the coming of the great Judge, "What ought you to be," says St. Peter to all the faithful, "And what ought to be the sanctity of your life, the piety of your actions, awaiting, and, as it were, hastening by your desires, the coming of the day of the Lord?" Jesus Christ, after having given a description of the frightful signs which will precede His coming, after having told us that men will wither away for fear in expectation of the evils with which the world of the impious will be threatened, addresses immediately to all His disciples who were present, and to all those who should follow Him during the course of ages, these sweet words of consolation and joy: "As for you, when these things begin to happen, look up, and lift up your heads, because your redemption is at hand. . . . When you shall see these things come to pass, know that the kingdom of God is nigh." The great maxims which the Apostles and Jesus Christ Himself teach us, accord perfectly with an ardent desire of death; but do they accord with an excessive fear of death? Are we not afraid to dishonor those great truths, by the opposition that we show between the dispositions which they require, and those which we entertain? "Jesus Christ," says St. Augustine, "will share His kingdom with all those who shall have sincerely desired that His kingdom should come." "He will render," says the Apostle, "the crown of justice to those who love His coming." What, then, should we desire more than His arrival, since it is the sure means of our reigning with Him?

Many persons are tormented at death with the remembrance of their crimes, and, seeing that they have done no penance, they are tempted to despair. "Oh, if I had fasted! Oh, if I had performed great charities for the poor! Alas! I am no longer in a state to perform them. What will become of me? What shall I do?" You can do something greater than all you have mentioned, namely, accept death, and unite it with that of Jesus Christ. There is no mortification comparable to this: it is the deepest humiliation, the greatest impoverishment, the most terrible penance; and I do not at all doubt but that he who is grieved for having offended God, and who accepts death willingly in satisfaction for his sins, will immediately obtain pardon. What a consolation to be able to perform while dying a greater penance than all the anchorets have been able to perform in deserts, and this at a time when one would seem no longer able to do anything! What a pity to see an innumerable multitude of persons deprive themselves of the fruit of death, which of all the pains of life is the one of most merit! *Ut quid perditio haec?*[6] Why waste so advantageous an occasion of honoring God, satisfying His justice, discharging one's debts, and purchasing Heaven?

I acknowledge that your life is nothing in comparison with that of Our Lord Jesus Christ; but, when offered through love, it is of inestimable value. What does God care about an alms of two farthings? Yet the poor widow, in the Gospel, who gave it, deserved to be praised by the Son of God, and to be preferred to the Scribes and Pharisees, who had given much more considerable alms, because, says He, she has given all that she had, and, notwithstanding her poverty, has given it with a great heart. *Haec de penuria*

6   "To what purpose is this waste?" (*Matt.* 26:8).—*Publisher, 2013.*

sua omnia quae habuit misit totum victum suum.[7]

We can say the same of him who gives his life to God: he gives all that he has, without reserving anything, and this is what renders death precious. This is what made the early Christians run with so much eagerness to martyrdom: they all wished to give back to Our Lord the life which they had received from Him, and to compensate by their death for that which He had endured for love of them.

We can no longer be martyrs; oh, what an affliction! But still we can die for Jesus Christ! We have a life that we can lose for His love! Oh, what a consolation!

The line of distinction which St. Augustine draws between the perfect and the imperfect is that the perfect suffer life with pain and receive death with joy, while the imperfect receive death only with patience, struggling against themselves to submit to the will of God: preferring however to yield to what He requires of them, arming themselves with courage to overcome the desire of life, and to receive death with submission and peace.

Perfection, therefore, consists in desiring to die, that we may no longer be imperfect, that we may wholly cease to offend God, that God may reign perfectly in us, and that this body of sin, which we carry about with us until death, may, in punishment of its continual revolts against God, be reduced to dust, fully to satisfy His justice and sanctity, and, by this last and most profound humiliation, fully to repair all the injuries which it has committed against the Divine Majesty. We rise towards perfection in proportion as these

---

7 "She of her want cast in all she had, even her whole living." (Cf. *Mark* 12:44). —*Publisher*, 2013.

holy desires of death become more ardent and sincere, and the quickest means of becoming perfect is to desire death with one's whole heart.

The preparations that we might wish to bring with us to our last sacrifice ought not, when the hour of consummating it arrives, to lead us to desire that the sacrifice should be deferred. These preparations are less necessary than submission to the will of God. Our submission can supply the place of these preparations, but nothing can supply the want of our submission; a thing which souls, even the most imperfect, should never forget. It is more advantageous for us to appear before Jesus Christ, when He announces His coming, than to expose ourselves to the risk of meeting Him too late, by expecting that we shall afterwards be better prepared. The essential preparation is to go before Him with confidence and love; and we must think only of exciting acts of these virtues. It ought to be a great subject of humiliation and confusion to us, not to feel a holy ardor and impatience to go to Him. Happy are we, says St. Chrysostom, if we sigh and groan continually within ourselves, awaiting the accomplishment of our divine adoption, which will be the redemption and deliverance of our bodies and souls—if we desire to depart from this world with as much ardor and impatience as the banished desire an end of their exile, and captives of their imprisonment.[8] This impatience, adds the holy doctor, which we testify to God, will serve much to obtain the pardon of our sins, and will be the best of all dispositions for appearing before Him.

---

8   Chrys., *Hom. xvii in Gen. et alib.*

We have elsewhere shown that no person, however holy his life may have been, should rely upon his virtues, if God should examine them without mercy. It is to be already condemned, to consent to be judged without a great mercy. Confidence in the divine mercy, and in the merits of Jesus Christ, is the only security for all. Since, then, we must always return to this point, let us, from this moment, abandon ourselves to these dispositions in life and in death. Let us hold, as a certain truth, that the more fully we thus abandon ourselves, the more just shall we be, and the more agreeable our sacrifices to God.